LIFE OF BEETHOVEN

ᴥ BOOKS FROM SEA RAVEN PRESS ᴥ

AMERICAN CIVIL WAR
Abraham Lincoln Was a Liberal, Jefferson Davis Was a Conservative: The Missing Key to Understanding
   the American Civil War
Confederacy 101: Amazing Facts You Never Knew About America's Oldest Political Tradition
Confederate Blood and Treasure: An Interview With Lochlainn Seabrook
Everything You Were Taught About African-Americans and the Civil War is Wrong, Ask a Southerner!
Everything You Were Taught About the Civil War is Wrong, Ask a Southerner!
Give This Book to a Yankee! A Southern Guide to the Civil War For Northerners
Lincoln's War: The Real Cause, the Real Winner, the Real Loser
The Great Yankee Coverup: What the North Doesn't Want You to Know About Lincoln's War!
The Ultimate Civil War Quiz Book: How Much Do You Really Know About America's Most
   Misunderstood Conflict?
Women in Gray: A Tribute to the Ladies Who Supported the Southern Confederacy

CONFEDERATE MONUMENTS
Confederate Monuments: Why Every American Should Honor Confederate Soldiers and Their
   Memorials

CONFEDERATE FLAG
Confederate Flag Facts: What Every American Should Know About Dixie's Southern Cross
What the Confederate Flag Means To Me: Americans Speak Out in Defense of Southern Honor,
   Heritage, and History

SECESSION
All We Ask Is To Be Let Alone: The Southern Secession Fact Book

SLAVERY
Everything You Were Taught About American Slavery is Wrong, Ask a Southerner!
Slavery 101: Amazing Facts You Never Knew About America's "Peculiar Institution"

CHILDREN
Honest Jeff and Dishonest Abe: A Southern Children's Guide to the Civil War
Saddle, Sword, and Gun: A Biography of Nathan Bedford Forrest For Teens

NATHAN BEDFORD FORREST
A Rebel Born: A Defense of Nathan Bedford Forrest - Confederate General, American Legend (winner
   of the 2011 Jefferson Davis Historical Gold Medal)
A Rebel Born: The Screenplay (film about N. B. Forrest)
Forrest! 99 Reasons to Love Nathan Bedford Forrest
Give 'Em Hell Boys! The Complete Military Correspondence of Nathan Bedford Forrest
I Rode With Forrest! Confederate Soldiers Who Served With the World's Greatest Cavalry Leader
Nathan Bedford Forrest and African-Americans: Yankee Myth, Confederate Fact
Nathan Bedford Forrest and the Battle of Fort Pillow: Yankee Myth, Confederate Fact
Nathan Bedford Forrest and the Ku Klux Klan: Yankee Myth, Confederate Fact
Nathan Bedford Forrest: Southern Hero, American Patriot - Honoring a Confederate Icon and the Old
   South
Saddle, Sword, and Gun: A Biography of Nathan Bedford Forrest For Teens
The God of War: Nathan Bedford Forrest As He Was Seen By His Contemporaries
The Quotable Nathan Bedford Forrest: Selections From the Writings and Speeches of the Confederacy's
   Most Brilliant Cavalryman

QUOTABLE SERIES
The Alexander H. Stephens Reader: Excerpts From the Works of a Confederate Founding Father
The Quotable Alexander H. Stephens: Selections From the Writings and Speeches of the Confederacy's
   First Vice President
The Quotable Jefferson Davis: Selections From the Writings and Speeches of the Confederacy's First
   President
The Quotable Nathan Bedford Forrest: Selections From the Writings and Speeches of the Confederacy's
   Most Brilliant Cavalryman
The Quotable Robert E. Lee: Selections From the Writings and Speeches of the South's Most Beloved
   Civil War General
The Quotable Stonewall Jackson: Selections From the Writings and Speeches of the South's Most
   Famous General
The Unquotable Abraham Lincoln: The President's Quotes They Don't Want You To Know!

CONSTITUTIONAL HISTORY
The Articles of Confederation Explained: A Clause-by-Clause Study of America's First Constitution
The Constitution of the Confederate States of America Explained: A Clause-by-Clause Study of the
   South's Magna Carta

Warning: SEA RAVEN PRESS BOOKS WILL EXPAND YOUR ★ MIND!

LIFE OF
BEETHOVEN

LUDWIG NOHL

Translated from the original German by John J. Lalor

"Our age has need of vigorous minds."

ORIGINALLY PUBLISHED IN 1881

THIS SPECIAL REPRINT EDITION EDITED, ILLUSTRATED, CAPTIONED, & ARRANGED BY AUTHOR-HISTORIAN

LOCHLAINN SEABROOK

JEFFERSON DAVIS HISTORICAL GOLD MEDAL WINNER

This is a Sea Raven Press Reprint

Not one word has been added to or subtracted from the original text

2021

Sea Raven Press, Nashville, Tennessee, USA

LIFE OF BEETHOVEN

Published by
Sea Raven Press, Cassidy Ravensdale, President
PO Box 1484, Spring Hill, Tennessee 37174-1484 USA
SeaRavenPress.com • searavenpress@gmail.com

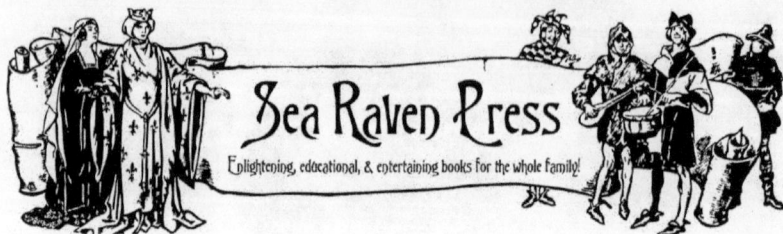

Sea Raven Press
Enlightening, educational, & entertaining books for the whole family!

Original text by Ludwig (Louis) Nohl (1831-1885)
This book was first published in 1881 by Jansen, McClurg & Co., Chicago, Illinois.
In our reprint not one word has been added to or subtracted from the original text.

1st SRP paperback edition, 1st printing, February 2021 • ISBN: 978-1-943737-96-3
1st SRP hardcover edition, 1st printing, February 2021 • ISBN: 978-1-943737-97-0

ISBN: 978-1-943737-96-3 (paperback)
Library of Congress Control Number: 2021932403

Life of Beethoven, by Ludwig Nohl (1880); translator John J. Lalor (1881); editor Lochlainn Seabrook (2021). This reprint edition published by Sea Raven Press (2021).

Front and back cover design and art, book design, layout, and interior art by Lochlainn Seabrook All images, graphic design, graphic art, illustrations, & captions copyright © Lochlainn Seabrook All images selected, placed, captioned, manipulated, and/or created by Lochlainn Seabrook Cover photo: "Concert Hall and Piano" by Serhii Khomiak

All persons who approve of the authority and principles of Sea Raven Press, and realize our benefits as a means of reeducating the world about authentic history, are hereby requested to avidly recommend our books to others and to vigorously cooperate in extending their reach, scope, and influence around the globe. Thank you.

SEA RAVEN PRESS

EDITOR'S DEDICATION

To Beethoven, my brother in spirit, with whom I share a love of God, nature, the piano, Old Europe, and 19th-Century music.

EDITOR'S EPIGRAPH

"Our very being and our sublimest feelings are touched when we hear the name of Ludwig van Beethoven."

Ludwig Nohl

PROFESSOR & BEETHOVEN SCHOLAR

1880

CONTENTS

"Bach: intricate, cerebral, precise, religious;
Mozart: melodic, playful, fluid, sensual;
Beethoven: masculine, emotional, impulsive, spiritual."

LOCHLAINN SEABROOK
Editor, 2021

NOTES TO THE READER

FAITHFULNESS TO NOHL'S & LALOR'S TEXT

☞ In order to preserve the integrity and authenticity of *Life of Beethoven*, I have retained Nohl's (the original German author) and Lalor's (the German-to-English translator) original spellings, formatting, and punctuation. These include such items as old German and English spellings, long-running paragraphs, obsolete words, outdated terms, unusual as well as ungrammatical hyphenations, capitalizations, and italicizations, and the many various literary devices peculiar to the European Victorian Era. Note that all parenthesized and bracketed words, notes, and sentences, are Nohl's (or Lalor's).

I have taken two liberties: 1) Where found I have corrected obvious typos; 2) Nohl's edition contained only one illustration (see the title page of this book). As I believe images add an important visual dimension, I have inserted additional photos and drawings that I feel augment Nohl's biographical material.

Concerning words specifically, however, none have been added, and none have been subtracted. The end result is an accurately rendered manuscript, one that carefully maintains every word of text from Nohl's original 1881 book—without the intrusive addition of modern redactions and commentary.

CONTINUE YOUR EDUCATION IN GENUINE HISTORY

☞ Western, and in particular both European and European American society, can never be fully understood without a basic knowledge of influential individuals from the past who helped create, develop, and sustain it. For those who are interested in additional material on these topics from the viewpoint of the American South, please see my comprehensive histories listed on pages 2 and 3.

THE AUTHOR'S
INTRODUCTION

MUSIC IS THE most popular of the arts. It fills man's breast with a melancholy joy. Even the brute creation is not insensible to its power. Yet, at its best, music is a haughty, exclusive being, and not without reason are training, practice, talent, and the development of that talent, required for the understanding of her secrets. "One wishes to be heard with the intellect, by one's equals; emotion becomes only women, but music should strike fire from the mind of a man." In some such strain as this, Beethoven himself once spoke, and we know how slowly the works of the great symphonist found a hearing and recognition from the general public.

Yet, who is there today who does not know the name of Beethoven? Who is there that, hearing one of his compositions, does not feel the presence of a sublime, all-ruling power—of a power that springs from the deepest sources of all life? His very name inspires us with a feeling of veneration, and we can readily believe the accounts that have come down to us; how even strangers drew back with a species of awe, before this man of imposing appearance, spite of his smallness of stature, with his rounded shoulders, erect head, wavy hair and piercing glance. Who has not heard of the two charcoal-burners who suddenly stopped their heavily laden vehicle when they met, in a narrow pass, this "crabbed musician," so well known to all Vienna, and who was wont to stand and think, and then, humming, to go his way, moving about bee-like through nature from sunrise, with his memorandum-book in his hand.

We are moved with the same feeling of respect that moved those common men, when we hear only Beethoven's name, but how much more powerfully are we stirred when we hear his music! We feel in that music the presence of the spirit that animates and sustains the world, and which is continually calling new life into existence. Even the person who is not a musician himself may feel, in these mighty productions, the certainty of the presence of the Creator of all things. Their tones sound to him like the voice of man's heart of hearts, the joys and sorrows of which Beethoven has laid bare to us. We feel convinced, when we hear them, that the person who in them speaks to us has, in very deed, something to tell us, something of our own life; because he lived and felt more deeply than we what we all live and feel, and loved and suffered what we all love and suffer, more deeply than any other child of dust. In Beethoven, we meet with a personage really great, both in mind and heart, one who was able to become a sublime model to us, because life and art were serious things with him, and one who made it his duty "to live not for himself, but for other men." The high degree of self-denying power found in this phenomenon of art, it is that has such an elevating effect on us. The duties of life and the tasks of the artist he discharged with equal fidelity. His life was the foundation on which the superstructure of his works rose. His greatness as a man was the source of his greatness as an artist. The mere story of his life, given here in outline, reveals to us the internal springs of his artistic creations, and we must perforce admit, that the history of Beethoven's life is a part of the history of the higher intellectual life of our time and of humanity.

LUDWIG NOHL
Germany, 1880

THE EDITOR'S
INTRODUCTION

THERE ARE MANY reasons for an author like me to undertake a reprint of a Victorian biography of Ludwig van Beethoven. To begin with, he is both one of the world's greatest European composers and one of my personal favorite composers from the Classical-Romantic Periods. And there are other reasons.

Beethoven and I are not only fellow composers of works such as symphonies, string quartets, piano sonatas, and choral pieces, but we are also both musicians. While Beethoven and I play multiple instruments, we are both most proficient on the piano. Beethoven and I write in many styles and for both instruments and voice. Lastly, Beethoven and I are professional composer-musicians who toured our respective countries performing our original music before live audiences.

Besides these numerous artistic similarities, Beethoven and I share Dutch and German heritage and strong national pride, as well as a passion for spirituality, the Great Outdoors, and individual freedom.

For me, if there were only one reason to resuscitate a 19th-Century Beethoven biography, however, it would be to help preserve the authentic history of Western society, which is being rewritten at a furious pace by the fact-loathing political Left. While Beethoven died in 1827, four years before the author was born (in 1831), Nohl recorded a myriad of details about Beethoven's life that could someday be lost. This little book will help prevent that possibility, while keeping this awe-inspiring composer in the public eye for centuries, even millennia, into the future.

Whatever one's personal estimation of the *man* whose name

literally translates as "Louis from the beet garden," it is his *music* that is most significant. We are fortunate indeed that it will live on forever through sheet music, as well as the recordings and live performances of modern day musicians, conductors, choirs, chamber groups, and orchestras.

If this book transforms one person who is unfamiliar with "the world's greatest composer" into a Beethoven disciple, my purpose in selecting, illustrating, and editing it will have been a success.

LOCHLAINN SEABROOK
Nashville, Tennessee, USA
February 2021
In Nobis Regnat Christus

CHAPTER I

BEETHOVEN'S YOUTH & EARLIEST EFFORTS

Birth and Baptism — His Family — Young Beethoven's Character — His Brothers Karl and Johann — Early Talent for Music — Appears in Public at the Age of Seven — Error as to His Age — Travels in Holland — Studies the Organ in Vienna — His Fame Foretold — His Personal Appearance — Meets Mozart — Mozart's Opinion of Him — Maximilian, Elector of Cologne, and Mozart — Beethoven's Intellectual Training — Madame von Breuning — First Love — Beethoven and Haydn — Compositions written in Vienna.

LUDWIG VAN BEETHOVEN was baptized in Bonn on the 17th of December, 1770. We know only this the date of his baptism, with any certainty, and hence the 17th of December is assumed to be his birthday likewise.

Beethoven's father, Johann van Beethoven. The family originated in the part of the Netherlands that is now Belgium. (Image/caption by the editor.)

His father, Johann van Beethoven, was a singer in the chapel of the Elector, in Bonn. The family, however, had come originally from the Netherlands. Beethoven's grandfather came to Bonn in 1732 after willfully leaving the parental roof in consequence of a quarrel. He had attracted attention as a bass singer in the church and the theater, and was made director of the court band in 1763. By his industry, he had founded a family, was earning a respectable livelihood, and had won for himself the personal regard of the community. He did, besides, a small business in wines, but this, which was only accessory to his calling as a musician, contributed to undermine both his own happiness and his son's. His wife, Josepha Poll, fell a victim to the vice of intemperance, and, in consequence, it at last became necessary to confine her in a convent in Cologne. Unfortunately, the only surviving son inherited the vice of his mother. "Johann van Beethoven was given to the tasting of wine from a very early age," says the account of his playmates. It was not long before this weakness got the upper hand to such an extent that his family and home suffered greatly. It finally led to his discharge from his position. Stephan van Breuning, our own Beethoven's friend in youth, saw him, on one occasion, liberate the drunken father out of the hands of the police in the public streets.

We here get a glimpse at a period in Beethoven's youth, which put the strength of his mind as well as the goodness of his heart to the test. For in consequence of the very respectable position occupied by his grandfather, of his own early appointment as court-organist, and of the rapid development of his talent, Beethoven soon enjoyed the society of the higher classes, and was employed in the capacity of musician in the families of the nobility and at court. Yet, we are told, whenever it happened that he and his two younger brothers were obliged to take their intoxicated father home, they always performed that disagreeable task with the utmost tenderness. He was never known to utter a hard or unkind word about the man who had made his youth so sunless, and he never failed to resent it when a third person spoke uncharitably of his father's frailty. The reserve and a certain haughtiness, however, which marked his disposition as a youth and a man, are traceable to these early harsh experiences.

And who knows the complications which caused misfortune to get the upper hand here! True, we are told that "Johann van Beethoven was of a volatile and flighty disposition;" but even his playmates, when he was a boy, had nothing bad to say of his character. Anger and stubbornness seem, indeed, to have been the inheritance of his Netherland nature; and these our hero also displayed to no small extent. But while the grandfather had earned a very good position for himself, and always so deported himself that young Beethoven might take him as an example, and loved to speak of him as a "man of honor," his father was never more than a singer in the chapel, on a small salary. But, notwithstanding his comparatively humble social position, he had made a mistake in marrying below his station.

Johann van Beethoven took Magdalena Kewerich, of Ehrenbreitstein, to wife, in 1763. She is described as a "pretty and slender woman." She had served as a chambermaid, for a time, in some of the families of the great, had married young, and was left a widow at the age of nineteen. Johann's marriage to this woman was not acceptable to the court *capellmeister*, and so it happened that he was obliged to leave the home in which he had thus far lived with his lonely father, and move into a wing of the house, number 515, in Bonn street, where his son Ludwig, the subject of this sketch, was born.

The young wife brought no property to her husband. Several children were born to the newly married couple in quick succession. Of these, Karl, born in 1774 and Johann in 1766, play some part in Beethoven's life. The growth of the

Beethoven's mother, Maria Magdalena Kewerich (also spelled Keverich). (Image/caption by the editor.)

family was so rapid that it was not long before they felt the burthen of pecuniary distress. The grandfather, who was well to do, helped them, at first. His stately figure in his red coat, with his massive head and "big eyes," remained fixed in the boy Ludwig's memory, although he was only three years of age when his grandfather died. The child was, indeed, tenderly attached to him. As the father's poverty increased, he made some efforts to improve his condition.

But they were of no avail; for his deportment was only "passable" and his voice "was leaving him." He now had recourse to teaching, and obtained employment in the theater, for he played the violin also. Sickness, however, soon eat up what was left of his little fortune. Their furniture and table ware followed their silver service and linen—"which one might have drawn through a ring,"—to the pawn-shop; and now the father's poverty contributed only to make him, more and more, the victim of his weakness for the cup.

But there was even now one star of hope in the dreary firmament of his existence—his son Ludwig's talent for music. This talent showed itself in very early childhood, and could not, by any possibility, escape the observation of the father, who, after all, was himself a "good musician." And, although the father was not destined to live to see his son in the zenith of his success, it was his son's talent alone that saved the family from ruin and their name from oblivion, for with the birth of Beethoven's younger brother, Johann, and of a sister who died shortly after, the circumstances of the family became still more straightened. Mozart had been in Bonn a short time before, and it occurred to the father to train his son to be a second little Mozart, and, by traveling with him, earn the means of subsistence of which the family stood so sorely in need. And so the boy was rigidly kept to his lessons on the piano and violin. His daily exercises on these instruments must have been a severer task on him than would seem to be necessary in a regular course of musical training. He used to be taken from his playing with other children to practice, and friends of his youth tell us how they saw him standing on a stool before the piano and cry while he practiced his lessons. Even the rod was called into requisition in his education, and the expostulations of friends could not dissuade the father from such relentless severity. But the end was attained. Regular and persevering exercise, laid the foundation of a skill in the art of music, which led him before the public when only seven years of age. On the 26th of March (by a strange coincidence the day of the month on which Beethoven died), the father announced, in a paper published in Cologne, that "his son, aged six years, would have the honor to wait on the public with several concertos for the piano, when, he flattered himself, he would be able to afford a distinguished audience a rich treat; and this all the more since he had been favored with a hearing by the whole court, who listened to him with the greatest pleasure." The child, to enhance the surprise, was made one year younger in this announcement than he was in reality; and this led Beethoven himself into an error as to his age, which he did not discover until he was nearly forty.

We need say but little concerning his other teachers when a youth. His great school was want, which urged him to follow and practice his art, so that he might master it, and, with its assistance, make his way through the world. When Beethoven grew to be eight years of age, he had as a teacher, in addition to his father, the vocalist Tobias Pfeiffer, for a whole year. Pfeiffer lived in the Beethoven family. He was a skillful pianist. Beethoven considered him one of the teachers to whom he was most indebted, and was subsequently instrumental in procuring assistance for him from Vienna. But we may form some idea of the nature of his instruction, and of the mode of living in the family, from the fact, attested by Beethoven's neighbors, that it frequently happened that Pfeiffer, after coming home with the father late in the night from the tavern, took young Ludwig out of bed and kept him at the piano practicing till morning.

Yet the success attendant on this instruction was such, even now, that when the boy, Beethoven and his teacher, who performed on the flute, played variations together, the people in the streets stopped and listened to their delightful music. In 1781, when Ludwig was ten years old, he traveled to Holland with his mother, played in the houses of the great, and astonished every one by his skill. The profits from this journey, however, cannot have been very large. When the boy was questioned about them, he replied: "The Dutch are a niggardly set; I shall never visit Holland again."

The house in which Beethoven was born.
(Image/caption by the editor.)

In the meantime, he turned his attention also to the study of the organ. Under the guidance of a certain Brother Willibald, of a neighboring Franciscan monastery, he soon became so proficient on that instrument, that he was able to act as assistant organist at divine service. But his principal teachers here were the old electoral court organist, van den Eeden, and afterwards, his successor, Christian Gottlob Neefe. In what regards composition the latter was the first to exercise any real influence on Beethoven, and Beethoven, in after years, thanked him for the good advice he had given him—advice which had contributed so much to his success in the "divine art." He concludes a letter to Neefe as follows: "If I should turn out some day to be a great man, you will have contributed to making me such." Neefe came originally from Saxony. As an organist, he had all the characteristics of the North German artists; but, on the other hand, he had, as a composer, a leaning towards the sonata-style introduced by Ph. E. Bach. He was a man of broad general education, and the form of his artistic productions was almost faultless. Such was young Beethoven's proficiency at the age of eleven, in 1782, that Neefe was able to appoint him his "substitute," and thus to pave the way for his appointment as court organist. We owe to him the first published account of Beethoven, and from that account we learn that the great foundation of his instruction was Bach's "well-tempered clavichord," that *ne plus ultra* of counterpoint and technic. He first made a reputation in Vienna by his masterly playing of Bach's fugues. But the instruction he had received in composition, bore fruit also, and some variations to a march and three sonatas, by him, appeared at this time in print.

In the account of Beethoven referred to above, and which was written in 1783, Neefe said that that young "genius" was deserving of support that he might be able to travel, and that he would certainly be another Mozart. But the development of his genius soon took a wider scope. He even, on one occasion, when Neefe was prevented doing so, presided at a rehearsal in the Bonn theater, in which the best pieces of the age were produced. This was at the age of twelve. And so it happened that his artistic views and technic skill grew steadily greater. We are told that when he became court organist, at the age of thirteen, he made the very accurate vocalist Heller lose the key entirely during the performance of divine service, by his own bold modulations. True, the Elector forbade such "strokes of genius" in the future, but he, no less than his *capellmeister* Luchesi, was greatly astonished at the extraordinary capacity of the young man.

Incidents of this kind may have suggested the propriety of giving him the instruction appropriate for a really great master of art; and, indeed, we find the court organist of Bonn with Mozart in Vienna, in the spring of 1787.

Beethoven's appearance was not what would be called imposing. He was small of stature, muscular and awkward, with a short snub nose. When he was introduced to Mozart, the latter was rather cool in his praise of his musical performances, considering them pieces learned by heart simply for purposes of parade. Beethoven, thereupon requested Mozart to give him a subject, that he might try his powers of musical improvisation. Charmed with the ability displayed in the execution of the task thus imposed on his young visitor, Mozart exclaimed: "Mark that young man the world will hear of him some day." Beethoven, however, received very little instruction from Mozart, who was so deeply engaged, just at this time, with the composition of his *Don Giovanni*, and so sorely tried by adverse circumstances, that he played very little for him, and could give him only a few lessons. Besides, Beethoven's mother was now taken seriously ill, and after a few weeks he had to return home, where other blows of a hard fate awaited him. His kind, good mother, was snatched from him by death, and his father's unfortunate weakness for strong drink obtained such a mastery over him that he was deprived of his position shortly after. The duty of supporting his two younger brothers was thus imposed on Ludwig, the eldest.

Young Beethoven was thus taught many a severe lesson early in life, in the hard school of adversity. But his trials were not without advantage to him. They gave to his character that iron texture which upheld him under the heaviest burthens, nor was his recall to Bonn a misfortune. He there found the very advantages which he had gone to seek in the musical metropolis, Vienna; for Maximilian Francis, Elector of Cologne, the friend and patron of Mozart, was one of the noble princes of the preceding century, who made their courts the sanctuary of culture and of art.

Maximilian was the youngest son of Maria Theresa. He had received the careful training, for which that imperial house was noted, and he found in Joseph II an example in every way worthy of imitation. He was as faithful to his calling as an ecclesiastic as to his duties as a ruler, and as adverse to what he looked upon as superstition in the garb of Christianity, as to the extravagance of his predecessors, who had left the country in a state of corruption and destitution. He everywhere endeavored to bring order out of chaos and to spread prosperity among his people. A pure, fresh atmosphere filled the little court as long as he presided in it. He was still young, not much over thirty, and a man of the truest principles. Speaking of him as "that most humane and best of princes," a contemporary writer says: "People had grown accustomed to think of Cologne as a land of darkness, but when they came to the Elector's court, they quickly changed their mind." The members of the orchestra of the court especially, among whom our young court organist is to be reckoned, were, we are told, very intelligent, right thinking men, of elegant manners and unexceptionable conduct.

The Elector had opened the University in 1776, and established a public reading-room, which he visited with no more ostentation than any one else. "All these institutions, as I looked upon it, had sworn allegiance to an unknown genius of humanity, and, for the first time in my life, my mind had a glimmer of the meaning and majesty of science," writes the painter, Gerhard Kuegelgen, and how could Beethoven have thought differently? He had, it is true, devoted himself so exclusively to music that he had made very little progress in anything else. In the use of figures he always found great difficulty, and his spelling was worse than could be easily tolerated even in his own day, when orthography was a rather rare accomplishment. He had studied a little

A silhouette of Beethoven in the year 1786, age 16. (Image/caption by the editor.)

French and Latin. But the breezes of a higher intellectual culture which, at this time, swept through Bonn and influenced him likewise through his intimate intercourse with the most highly cultivated people of the city, soon lifted him to heights unattained by other artists and musicians of his century—heights from which he continually discerned new fields of action. As a consequence of this intercourse with the learned, he acquired intellectual tastes in various directions, and so seriously occupied himself with things intellectual that they became a necessity to his nature. He tells us himself that, without laying the least claim to real learning, it had been his endeavor from childhood to acquaint himself with what was best and wisest in every age. But these intellectual leanings did not prevent him from being, as the painter Kuegelgen said of himself, lovingly devoted to his art. And his own beloved art of music was, at this very time, cultivated in Bonn with a greater earnestness and devotion than any other.

The writer referred to above, speaking of the Elector, says: "Not only did he play himself, but he was an enthusiastic lover of music. It seemed as if he could never tire of hearing it. Whenever he went to a concert, he was the most attentive person in the whole audience." And no wonder; for the musical instruction given to the children of Maria Theresa was excellent. Indeed, the art of music in Vienna was at that time at its height. That city was the scene of the labors of Gluck, Haydn and Mozart. And so there was only good music to be heard in the "cabinet" at Bonn. Our Beethoven, now a distinguished pianist, contributed his share to this; and we need not be surprised to find him employed by a prince who knew Mozart and loved him.

But it was not musicians alone who were benefited by prince's patronage. No sooner did the condition of the country leave him the necessary leisure, and the state of its finances afford him the necessary means, than he turned his best attention to the theater and the orchestra. As far back as 1784, Maximilian Francis had organized an orchestra, and our young court organist took a place in it as a player of the tenor violin. The violinist, Ries, and Simrock, a performer on the French horn, were also members of it. Ries and Simrock had henceforth much to do with Mozart. The following year, a troupe visited Bonn, and gave Italian operas, French vaudevilles, as well as Gluck's *Alceste and Orpheus*. They were followed by Grossmann, a person of rare intellect, and one who holds a distinguished place in the history of German dramatic art. His repertory included the plays of Shakespeare, Lessing, Schiller and Goethe, with all of whom Beethoven thus became acquainted early in life. In 1788, Maximilian Francis established a national theater, and, dating from this, dramatic poetry and music began to flourish in Bonn, so that it took its place, in this respect, side by side with Mannheim, Vienna and Weimar, and became a school well calculated to foster the great abilities of Beethoven. In the orchestra we find such men as Andreas, Bernhard Romberg and Anton Reicher, afterwards so celebrated as a writer on the theory of music. The latter was, at this time, Beethoven's most intimate friend and companion in art. Actors, too, come upon the stage, many of whom subsequently filled all Germany with their fame. Dramatic works of every description appeared. There was Martin's *Tree of Diana*, Mozart's *Elopement from the Seraglio*, Salieri's *Grotto of Trophonius*, Dittersdorf's *Doctor and Apothecary*, and *Little Red Riding Hood*, Gluck's *Pilgrim of Mecca*, besides Paisiello's *King Theodore*, and greatest of all, *Don Giovanni*. The music "pleased connoisseurs;" and *Figaro's Marriage* greatly charmed both singers and the members of the orchestra, who vied with one another to do justice to that beautiful opera. "The strength of our theater," says a writer of the time, characteristically and simply, "lay in our opera."

This continual contemplation of "characters in tone" played a decided part in the development of an artist who was destined to infuse into instrumental music so much of poetical and even of dramatic life. We are informed that Beethoven's power of delineating character in the language of music was so great, even at this time, that when improvising, which he was very fond of doing, he was frequently asked "to describe the character of some well known person." One distinguishing peculiarity of the Bonn orchestra had a marked influence in the development of the great symphonist of the future, Beethoven. We refer to what has been called "the accurate observation of musical light and shade, or of the *forte* and *piano*." This musical peculiarity was introduced into the Bonn orchestra by a former *capellmeister*, Mattioli, "a man full of fire and refined feeling," who had learned orchestral accentuation and declamation from Gluck, and whose musical enthusiasm caused him to be considered the superior of Cannabich of Mannheim, who played such a part in Mozart's life, and who had originated this mode of musical delivery in Germany. He was succeeded by Joseph Reicha, under whose energetic leadership the Bonn orchestra reached its highest point of perfection. In the autumn of 1791, we find that entire orchestra in Mergentheim, the seat of the German order of which Maximilian Francis was Grand Master; and we have an account of it from Mergentheim which gives us a very clear idea of Beethoven's life as a student. Our informant tells us, in the first place, that he was very much impressed by an octett of wind instruments. All eight players were, he says, masters who had reached a high degree of truth and perfection, especially in the sustaining of tones. Does not this remind one of Beethoven's exquisite septett op. 20? How Ries infused life and spirit into all by his sure and vigorous bowing in the orchestra! What once could be heard only in Mannheim, we are told, was now heard here—the close observance of the *piano* and the *forte* and the *rinforzando*, the swell and gradual growth of tone, followed by the dropping of the same from the utmost intensity to the merest breath. Bernhard Romberg's playing is lauded for "perfection of expression and its fine shades of feeling which appeal to the heart;" his cousin Andreas's for "taste in delivery," and the true art of his "musical painting." Can we wonder that Beethoven's emulation of, and struggling for the mastery with such men contributed constantly to develop his genius? He is praised for the peculiar expression of his playing, and above all for the speaking, significant, expressive character of his fancy. Our informant says, in closing his account: "I found him wanting in nothing which goes to make the great artist. All the superior performers of this orchestra are his admirers. They are all ears when he plays, but the man himself is exceedingly modest and without pretension of any kind."

We have now seen what was Beethoven's technical training both by practice and example, on the organ and the piano, in the theater and the orchestra, and how all these were to him a school of musical composition; for the Bonn orchestra was as conversant with Mozart and Haydn as we of today are with Beethoven. How thoroughly he comprehended and appreciated Mozart especially, is attested by what he once said to John Cramer, the only piano-player to whom Beethoven himself applied terms of high praise. The two were walking, in 1799, in the park in Vienna, listening to Mozart's concert in C minor. "Cramer! Cramer!"

Beethoven exclaimed, when he heard the simple and beautiful theme near the close: "We shall never be able to accomplish anything like that." "What a modest man!" was the reply. This leads us to say something of the few beautiful, purely human gifts which were the fruit Beethoven enjoyed through life, of his youth in Bonn.

In Bonn, lived Madame von Breuning, with her four children, who were only a little younger than our court-organist. Beethoven and one of the sons, Stephan, received instruction in music from Ries, and were thus thrown together. But it was not long before our young artist himself was called upon to teach the piano in the family of Madame von Breuning. How lonely Beethoven felt after his good mother had succumbed to her many sufferings and sorrows, we learn from the first letter of his that has come down to us. We there read: "She was so good and amiable a mother to me! She was my best friend. O, who was happier than I while I could yet pronounce the sweet name of mother! There was once some one to hear me when I said 'mother!' But to whom can I address that name now? Only to the silent pictures of her which my fancy paints." But Madame von Breuning became a second mother to him; and what her home was, we are informed by Doctor Wegeler, afterwards husband of Madame von Breuning's daughter Eleonore, for a time one of Beethoven's pupils. He writes: "Her home was pervaded by an atmosphere of unconstrained refinement, spite of an occasional outburst of the petulance of youth." The boy, Christoph, took very early to the writing of little poems. Stephan did the same thing at a much later date, and successfully. The useful and agreeable were found combined in the little social entertainments of family friends. It was not long before Beethoven was treated as one of the children. He spent the greater part of the

Beethoven in the year 1791, at the age of 21. (Image/caption by the editor.)

day in Madame Bruening's home, and not unfrequently, the night. He felt at home in the family, and everything about him contributed to cheer him and to develop his mind." When it is known, on the authority of the same Doctor Wegeler, that it was at Madame von Breuning's home that Beethoven first became acquainted with German literature, that there he received his first lessons in social etiquette, it is easy to estimate the value to him of the friendship of the Breuning family—a friendship which was never interrupted for a moment during his long life.

It was while in the enjoyment of this intercourse with the Breuning family that he felt the first charming intimations of the tender passion. Wegeler makes mention of two young ladies, one of whom, a pretty, cheerful and lively blonde, Jeannette d' Honrath, of Cologne, was a frequent visitor at the Breuning's. She took delight in teasing our young musician, and playfully addressed him, singing:

> "Mich heute noch von dir zu trennen,
> Und dieses nicht verhindern koennen,
> Ist zu empfendlich für mein herz!"[1]

His favored rival in Jeannette's affections was a captain in the Austrian army, by the name of Greth. His name occurs, in 1823, in the written conversations of our deaf master. He was just as much taken with the sweet and beautiful Miss W. (Westherhold), but to no purpose. He called his love for her a "young Werther's love," and, many years after, he told B. Romberg a great many anecdotes about it. What he thought of his acquaintance with the Breuning family and these two young persons may be inferred from the words in which he dedicated the variations *Se vuol ballare*, to his friend Lorchen (Eleonore Breuning) in 1793: "May this work," he says, "serve to recall the time when I spent so many and such happy hours in your home."

---

1. "To part from thee, my dear, this day, And know that I can't with thee stay, Is more than my sad heart can bear."

Besides the home of the Breunings, in which Beethoven was always so welcome, we may mention another—that of Count Waldstein, to whom the sonata op. 23 is dedicated. The count was very friendly to Beethoven. He was aware of his genius, and, on that account, afforded him pecuniary assistance. Yet, to spare the artist's feelings, this assistance was made to have the appearance of coming from the Elector. It may be that it was this same amiable and art-loving young Austrian who endeavored to keep Beethoven's eye fixed on the one place in the world in which he could receive the final touch to his musical education,—Vienna. The very multitude of Beethoven's ideas, and the height to which his intellect had soared, showed him that he was far from having reached perfection in the artistic representation of those ideas. His readiness of execution and his wonderful power of improvisation, even now, assured him victory wherever he went. But the small number of compositions which he wrote at this time, in Bonn, is sufficient proof that he did not feel sure of himself as a composer. And yet he had now reached an age at which Mozart was celebrated as a composer of operas.

In March, 1790, Haydn, on his journey to London, passed through Bonn, and was presented to the orchestra by Maximilian Francis, in person. He returned in the summer of 1792, and as Mozart had died in the meantime, nothing was more natural than that Beethoven should apply to the greatest living musician for instruction. The Elector assisted him; and we may divine how the young musician's heart must have swelled, now that he had

Beethoven in the year 1796, age 26. (Image/caption by the editor.)

entered the real wrestling-place in his art, from what, as we stated before, he said to his teacher Neefe : "If I ever become a great man," etc. But what was there that is not expected from such a person? Waldstein expressed the "realization of his long contested wishes" by writing in Beethoven's album: "By uninterrupted industry, thou wilt acquire the mind of Mozart from the hands of Haydn." When the wars of the Revolution swept over the boundaries of France, the excitement produced was great and universal. Beethoven was affected only by its ideal side. He was spared the sight of the grotesque ridiculousness of the *sans culottes* and the blood of the guillotine. After a short journey, in November, 1792, Vienna afforded him a safe retreat which he never afterwards left. It was not long before the French were masters of the Rhine. Maximilian Francis was obliged to flee, and thus every prospect of Beethoven's returning home was lost.

It now became imperative that he should take care of himself. His two brothers were provided for—Karl was a musician and Johann an apothecary. They soon followed him to Vienna, where it was not long before they renewed the scenes of his home life in Bonn. But his own constant endeavor was to be the creative artist that, as he became more firmly convinced every day, he was born to be. His studies under Haydn, then under Schenk, with whom the readers of the *Life of Mozart* are familiar from his connection with the opera of the *Magic Flute*, afterwards under the dry-as-dust Albrechtsberger, the teacher of counterpoint, and even under Mozart's deadly enemy, Salieri—were earnestly and zealously pursued, as is evident from what he has left after him. But even now his mind was too richly developed and his fancy too lofty to learn anything except by independent action. Ten of Beethoven's works date from the time he lived in Bonn; but, during his first sojourn in Vienna, compositions flowed in profusion from his pen, and we cannot but suppose that the germs of many of these last were sown during the period of his virtuosoship in Bonn. We conclude this chapter with a list of the works here referred to.

Besides his first attempts at musical composition already mentioned, a concerto for the piano written in 1784, and three quartets for the piano written in 1785, which were afterwards made use of in the sonatas op. 2, we must add, as certainly dating from this period of Beethoven's life in Bonn, a ballet by Count Waldstein (1791), a trio for the piano in E flat, the eight songs of op. 52, which appeared in 1805, two arias, one of which occurs in this op. as Goethe's *Mailied*, a part of the Bagatellen op. 33 which appeared in 1803, the two preludes op. 39, a minuet published in 1803, the variations *Vieni Amore* (1790), a funeral cantata on the death of Joseph II (1790), and one on that of Leopold II

Ludwig van Beethoven (1712-1773), Beethoven's grandfather and namesake. (Image/caption by the editor.)

(1792), the last of which was submitted to Haydn and which he thought a great deal of—both of these latter compositions are lost—an allegro and minuet for two flutes, a rondino for reed instruments and the string trio op. 3 which appeared in 1796.

In addition to these, there are, in all probability, many other compositions which were completed during Beethoven's first sojourn in Vienna, and published at a still later date; the octet op. 103, after which the quintet op. 4 was patterned before 1797, the serenade op. 8, which contained the germ of his nocturne op. 42; the Variations op. 66, on *Ein Maedchen oder Weibohen*, from the *Magic Flute* (published in 1798); the variations on *God Save the King*, the Romance for the violin, both of which appeared in 1805, when Beethoven's brother secretly published much of his music; the variation on *Se Vuol Ballare* from Mozart's *Figaro*; the *Es War Einmal* from Dittersdroff's *Little Red Riding Hood*, the "See He Comes," the Messias, and a theme by Count Waldstein (appeared 1793, 1797), the *Easy Sonata* in C major, dedicated to Eleonore von Breuning; the prelude in F minor (appeared in 1805), and the sextet for wind instruments, op. 71, which appeared in 1810.

In his twenty-third year, Mozart could point to three hundred works which he had composed, among them the poetical Sonatas

of his youth. How little of sunshine and leisure must there have been in a life which, spite of its extraordinary intellectual wealth and activity, reaped so little fruit! And even if we fix the date when the three trios op. 1, were composed in this period, when Beethoven was for the first time taught the meaning of the world and history, by the stormy movements of the last decade of the last century; and admit that the two concertos for the piano (op. 19 and op. 15) owe their origin to the wonderful fantasias with which he charmed the hearts and minds of the people of Bonn at that time, yet how little did he achieve! This fact is the most convincing proof of the truth of Beethoven's own assertion, that fortune did not favor him in Bonn. Leaving his musical training out of consideration, Beethoven's youth was not a very happy one. Seldom was it brightened for any length of time by the smiles of joy.

CHAPTER II

T HE GOLDEN AGE of music in Vienna had not passed away
when Beethoven came to that city. Not the court, but the
wealthy nobility, and a great many circles of the cultured
found in music the very soul of their intellectual life and of a nobler
existence. A consequence of this was that more attention was paid
to chamber music than any other; and we accordingly find that the
greater number of Beethoven's compositions, written at this
period, are of that style of music. Their very dedications tell us
much of the social circles of Vienna, and of the persons who graced
them.

First of all, we have the three trios op. 1, dedicated to Prince
Karl von Lichnowsky. The man who had been the pupil and friend
of Mozart might be glad, indeed, to see a substitute found so soon
for that departed genius. A quartet consisting of the able artists
Schuppenzigh, Sina, Weiss and Kraft, played at his house every
Friday. Dr. Wegeler informs us that Beethoven, in 1794, lived with

The organ at the Monastery of the Minorites in Bonn, Germany, where Beethoven first learned to play music. (Image/caption by the editor.)

the Prince, who, at a later date, paid him a salary of twelve hundred marks. The variations on *Seht er Kommt*, ("See He Comes") 1797, were dedicated to his consort, the Princess Christiane, *nee* Thun. She prized Beethoven very highly, and, as he once said of her himself, would have liked to encase him in glass, that he might be screened from the defiling breath and touch of the unworthy. The first three sonatas op. 2 are dedicated to J. Haydn, and they introduce us to his special patron, the Prince Esterhazy, with whom Beethoven was not very intimate, although the commission to write the mass op. 86 was given by Nicholas Esterhazy. The quartet op. 4, as well as the sonatas for violin, op. 23 and 24 (1800), and the string quintet op. 29 (1801), are dedicated to Count Fries. There is much in Beethoven's life to show that he was on terms of close friendship with this rich "merchant." The sonata op. 7 (1797), is dedicated to Countess Keglevics. The first concerto, which was finished in 1794, is dedicated to the same person, then known as Princess Odescalchi. The trios op. 9, as well as the brilliant sonata op. 22, belong, by right of dedication, to the Russian Count Browne, whom Beethoven himself called *le premier Mecene de sa muse*, and the sonatas op. 10 (1798), to his consort. To the Countess von Thun, he dedicated the trio op. 11, composed the same year, and the sonatas op. 12, to Salieri, one of his teachers in Vienna.

How highly Beethoven esteemed Lichnowsky is evidenced by the dedication to him of op. 14, the *Pathetique* (1799). In it we find the earliest expression of Beethoven's view of music as a voice speaking to man's innermost nature, calling to him to live a higher life. To Lichnowsky, likewise, was dedicated the sonata op. 26 with the beautiful funeral march (1802). The two lovely sonatas op. 14 of the year 1799, as well as the sonata for the horn, op. 17 (1800), are dedicated to the Countess Braun, whose husband gave Beethoven, some years after, the commission for the *Fidelio*; and the quintet op. 16 which was finished in 1797 to Prince Schwarzenberg. When we connect the name of Prince Lobkowitz with the first quartets op. 18, composed in 1797-1800; that of Baron von Swieten the lover of the well-tempered clavichord with the first symphony op. 21 (1800), that of the learned von Sonnenfels with the so-called pastoral sonata op. 28 (1801), we can see the force of the remark made by J. F. Reichart, that the Austrian nobility of this period loved and appreciated music better probably than any other in the history of the world. That they did not continue to do so is due entirely to the fact of the general disturbance of their pecuniary circumstances consequent on the wars which came to an end only in 1815, and which diminished their favorable influence on the cultivation of the art of music. But our artist had all the advantages of this noble patronage. He spared no pains nor sacrifice to profit by it. But his mind could not rest in the mere enjoyment of music. It sought other and higher spheres. His art was destined to absorb into itself the whole world of culture, to take an active part in the march of history and co-operate in giving expression to the ideas of life. The first real exploits of our artist were the *Eroica* and the *Fidelio* with the Leonore overture; but the path which led to them was one on which those immediately surrounding him could not very well follow him, and one which subsequently isolated him personally more and more from his fellow men.

It was an ill-defined longing for this starry path of a higher intellectual existence which brought him to the north of Germany, to Berlin, after he had finished the principal parts of the course in music under Haydn, Schenk and Albrechtsberger. Not that he did not meet with recognition and remuneration in his new home. But, after all, the recognition and remuneration he met with there were such as a virtuoso might expect. For the present, neither the public nor music publishers would have much to do with his compositions. Writing to Schiller's wife, the young Bonn professor, Fischenich, says of him: "So far as my acquaintance with him goes, he is made for the great and the sublime. Haydn has said that he would give him great operas, and soon be compelled himself to stop composing." He informs her, at the same time, that Beethoven was going to set her husband's Hymn to Joy—*Freude choener Goetterfunken*—to music. We thus see that he, even now, harbored those great ideas which engaged him at the close of his labors, in the composition of the Ninth Symphony. There were as yet but few traces to be found in Vienna of the intellectual awakening to which Germany is indebted for its earliest classical literature, and the period of its great thinkers in the west and the north. On the other hand, Beethoven's own mind was too full of the "storm and stress" to be able to appreciate the beautiful harmony and the warmth which had made such phenomena as Haydn and Mozart possible in South-German Austria. But in the North, the memory of "old Fritz" still lived; there the stern rule of mind and conscience, generated by Protestantism, still prevailed, while the firm frame-work of his own art, the counterpoint of the great Bach, the "first father of harmony," as he calls him himself, was there preserved, apparently, in its full strength. In addition to all this, the court there was fond of music, and King Frederick William II had endeavored to keep Mozart, the greatest master of his time, in Berlin; while Beethoven, since the Elector's flight from Bonn, had no further prospects in his home on the Rhine. He, therefore, decided to remove to the North.

We find him on his journey thither at the beginning of 1796. "My music secures me friends and regard—what more do I want?" he writes from Prague to his brother Johann, who, in the meantime, had entered into the employment of an apothecary in

The title page of Beethoven's first printed compositions, published circa 1781. He was 11 years old at the time. The music was dedicated to Archbishop and Elector of Cologne Maximilian Friedrich. (Image/caption by the editor.)

Vienna. He here composed the aria *Ah Perfido* (op.65). On his way to Berlin he passed through Dresden and Leipzig, but of his stay in these two cities, we have no information. The king received him very graciously; he played a few times at court and composed the sonatas for cello, op. 5, because the king himself played the violincello. The very first impression received by Beethoven seems to have been decisive. K. Ezerny, to whom he taught the piano, tells us something from his own recollection and observation about him, which is very characteristic of the man, and shows how sorely disappointed he felt in his most ardent expectations in Berlin. He says: "His improvisation was very brilliant, astonishing in the highest degree . . . . No matter in what society he was thrown, he made such an impression on all his hearers that it frequently happened that not a dry eye was to be seen, while many broke into sobs. There was something wonderful in his expression, besides the beauty and originality of his ideas, and the highly intellectual way he had of presenting them. When he had finished an improvisation of this kind he could break out into a fit of loud laughter and ridicule his hearers on the emotions he had excited. At times he even felt injured by those signs of sympathy. "Who," he asked, "can live among such spoiled children?" and for that reason alone he once declined an invitation extended to him by the king of Prussia, after an improvisation of this kind.

Beethoven was doomed to a disappointment of a very peculiar

kind here. Instead of the manliness of character which he, coming from the softer South, expected to find in the North, he was confronted with a voluptuous luxury to which his art was only a handmaid, and with an apparent surfeit of music, the natural outgrowth of the French influence due to Voltaire's residence in Berlin. Such was not the spirit of the new era which animated himself, and for the operation of which he was seeking a proper theater of action. The king himself did all in his power to make Gluck and Mozart settle in Berlin, and Handel's Oratorios were played even at the court concerts. But how could a man like Beethoven have worked side by side with the ruling leaders in music—with a Himmel and a Rhigini? The only person in Berlin who seemed to Beethoven a man, in the full sense of the word, was Prince Louis Ferdinand. With genuine frankness, he remarked of the prince's playing that "it was not kingly or princely, but only that of a good piano player." But it is probable that from the prince he borrowed the chivalric and, at the same time, poetico-enthusiatic character found in his third concerto (op. 37), which was finished in 1800 and dedicated to the prince, "the most human of human beings."

He played twice in the Singing Academy before its conductor, Fasch, and his successor, Zelter, Goethe's well-known friend, when he again brought the tears to the eyes of his hearers. But he clearly saw from the example of these two principal representatives of the more serious taste for music in Berlin, that it was not Bach's spirit which he was in search of that ruled there, but only a caricature of it; and this last was by no means a counterpoise to the Italian style of music, which still held absolute sway. He returned to Vienna disappointed in every respect, but with all the greater confidence in himself. He never again left Austria for good. It became the scene of his grandest achievements, and it was not long before their history began.

In a small memorandum book used by Beethoven on his journey from Bonn to Vienna, we find the following passage: "Take courage. Spite of all physical weakness, my mind shall rule. I have reached my twenty-fifth year, and must now be all that I can be. Nothing must be left undone." The father always represented Beethoven to be younger than he really was. Even in 1810, the son would not admit that he was forty years of age. The words quoted above must, therefore, have been written in the winter of 1796 or 1797; and this fact invests them with a greater significance than they would otherwise possess; for our artist now saw that, without the shadow of a doubt, Austria and Vienna were to be his abiding places; and he, therefore, strained every nerve, regardless of what the consequences might be, "to be a great man sometime;" that is, to accomplish something really good in music. This regardlessness of consequences manifested itself especially in the little care he seemed to take of his physical well-being. A friend, who had every opportunity to observe him, Baron von Zmeskall, informs us that "in the summer of 1796, he came home almost overpowered by the heat, tore open the doors and windows of the house, took off his coat and vest and seated himself at an open window to cool himself. The consequence of his imprudence was a dangerous illness, which ultimately settled on the organs of hearing. From this time his deafness kept on increasing." It is possible that the first symptoms of his deafness did not appear as early as 1796; but certain it is, that it dates back into the last decade of the last century, that it was brought about by heedlessness of his health, and that it became a severe tax on his moral courage. His genius was so absorbed in his music, that he too frequently forgot to take care of the physical man. In November, 1796, Stephan von Breuning remarked of him, that "his travels had contributed to mature his character; that he was a better judge of men, and had learned to appreciate the value, but, at the same time, the rarity of good friends." The hard trials of life had added to the earnestness of his disposition, and he was awakening to a full sense of what his own duty in this world was. This leads us to the first great and memorable work of his genius—to the *Eroica*, followed soon after by the symphony in C minor.

When, in the year 1806, one of his friends informed Beethoven of Napoleon's victory at Jena, he exclaimed: "It's a pity that I do not understand the art of war as well as I do the art of music. If I did I certainly would conquer him." These words express a rivalry almost personal in its nature, and could have been spoken only by a fool or by a man of power not unlike that of Napoleon himself.

And, indeed, leaving out of consideration men of genius like Goethe and Schiller, whose fame had been long established on a firm foundation, there were among his contemporaries men of sovereign ambition, only one person, Napoleon Bonaparte, able to make any great impression on a man who had chosen for his motto: "Power is the moral code of men who distinguish themselves above others; and it is mine, too." A series of the most brilliant victories was achieved up to 1798 by the General of the glorious French Republic,

Countess Giulietta Guicciardi. (Image/caption by the editor.)

who was of the same age as Beethoven. General Bernadotte, whose descendants occupy the throne of Sweden in our day, had participated in those victories. Bernadotte was the French Ambassador to Vienna in the beginning of 1798. He was young; by his origin he belonged to the middle class; he was the representative of the Republic, and could, therefore, indulge, unconstrained, in personal intercourse with whomsoever he pleased.

The celebrated violinist, Rudolph Kreutzer, to whom Beethoven's *Kreutzer Sonata* (op. 47) is dedicated, was one of his retinue. It was very natural that once Bernadotte and Kreutzer became acquainted with Beethoven, their intercourse with him and their friendship for him, should have been more than usually intimate. Bernadotte, who was sincerely devoted to Napoleon, and who must have felt himself drawn still more closely to Beethoven, because of his enthusiasm for the general, suggested to him the idea of celebrating the exploits of his hero by a symphony. Beethoven so informed his amanuensis, Schindler, in 1823, and his account is corroborated by other facts, that such was the first impulse to the composition of the *Eroica*.

But the advocate of power was destined soon to swell to the proportions of the hero of intellectual courage. "For thus does fate knock at the gates." Beethoven used these words in 1823, in speaking "with uncontrollable enthusiasm" of that wonderful *motive* at the opening of the symphony in C minor. The last movement of the work, the fanfare-like *finale*, so expressive of the joy of victory, shows that he here described a victory indeed, the surmounting of the obstacles and darkness of life, even if those obstacles and that darkness consisted only of "the infirmities of the body." The sketches of this movement, however, occur in the draft of the quartet op. 18, and hence must have been noted down before the year 1800! But the fact that the melody of the *adagio* was also found in that sketch shows that he was even then as certain of mastering sorrow, as he was conscious of the presence of the "demon in his ears," and of the sad prospect of a "wretched" and lonely future—a prospect which stirred him to the very depths of his soul.

But it was years before these motives took shape in his mind. To do justice to the great ideas to which they give expression, to the heroic victory of power and will over whatever opposes them, he had to concentrate and strengthen all his powers of mind and heart, and to develop his talents by long exercise. The portraiture of the struggles and of the artistic creations of the next succeeding years constitutes the transition to those first great heroic deeds—a transition which must be understood by all who would understand Beethoven's music.

The Napoleonic way in which Beethoven, at the close of the last century, outgeneraled all the most celebrated virtuosos of the time in Vienna and in Europe, is attested by his triumph over the renowned pianist Woelff, in 1799, and his defeat of Steibelt, in 1800. But he did still more towards achieving success by his works. His numerous variations won over to him many a fair player of the piano, while his *Adelaide*, which appeared in 1797, gained for him the hearts of all persons of fine feeling; so that Wegeler may have told the simple truth, when he wrote: "Beethoven was never, at least so long as I lived in Vienna (1794–96), without a love affair; and he occasionally made a conquest which it would have been very hard, if not impossible, for many a handsome Adonis to have made." The "ugly," pock-marked man, with the piercing eyes, was possessed of a power and beauty more attractive than any mere physical charms. And then, there was the charm of his sonatas: op. 7, with the funeral song in *adagio*, which he is said to have written in a tempest of "passionate feeling"; of op. 10, with its genuine masculine profile; of the revolutionary sonata in C minor, with the mysterious struggle in the *allegretto* in No. II, and the brilliant exultation of victory in the *allegro* in No. III, the tragic song of the *largo*, the gentle grace of the minuet—here used exceptionally in the place of the *scherzo*, as we find it already in op. 1; and, last of all, the droll question of little Snub Nose, in the *finale*. And yet these were followed by the *Pathetique*, with its exquisite and enrapturing *adagio*, and the two beautiful love songs, op. 14; by the six quartets, op. 18, in which he offered to a society of friends of his art, true songs of the soul and pictures of life overflowing; by the *adagio* of No. I, another Romeo-and-Juliet grave scene; by the *adagio* of No. VI, descriptive of the melancholy which, even now, began to gather its dark clouds about Beethoven himself, whose breast was so well attuned to joy. The descriptive septet (op. 20, 1800,) and the first symphony (op. 21), sketched after the style of Haydn, but painted with Mozart's pencil, are the last scenes in what we may call Beethoven's older life, which closed with the eighteenth century. The beginning of the nineteenth opened a new world to our artist.

The new world thus opened to Beethoven, and the manner in

which he himself conceived it, may be best described in Schiller's magnificent verses :

"Wie shön, O Mensch, mit deinem Palmenzweige
Stehst du an des Jahrhunderts Neige,
In edler stolzer Männhichkeit!
Mit aufgeschlossnem Sinn, mit Geistesfülle,
Voll milden Ernsts, in thatenreicher Stille,
Der reifste Sohn der Zeit.
Frei durch Vernunft, stark durch Gesetze,
Durch Sanftmuth gross und reich durch Schätze,
Die lange Zeit dein Busen dir verschewieg."

And now began for Beethoven a period of severe trials, brought upon him by himself. Absorbed in work, he neglected to take sufficient care of his physical health. His trouble with his hearing was increasing, but he paid no attention to it. His carelessness in this regard reduced him to a condition in which he would have found no alleviation and no joy, were it not for the inexhaustible resources he possessed within himself. But to understand him fully, we must read what he wrote himself, in June, 1801, to the "best of human kind," his friend Amenda, in Kurland, who had left Vienna two years before. He says:

"Your own dear Beethoven is very unhappy. He is in conflict with nature and with God. Many and many a time have I cursed Him because He has made His creatures the victims of the smallest accidents in nature, and this to such an extent that what promises to be best and most beautiful in life, is destroyed. You must know that what was most precious to me, my hearing, has been, in great part, lost. How sad my life is! All that was dear to me, all that I loved is gone! How happy would I now be, if I could only hear as I used to hear! If I could, I would fly to thee; but as it is, I must stay away. My best years will fly, and I shall not have fulfilled the promise of my youth, nor accomplish in my art what I fondly hoped I would. I must now take refuge in the sadness of resignation."

Beethoven's watch. (Image/caption by the editor.)

We have here the words to the long-drawn funereal tones of a song as we find it at the beginning of the celebrated C sharp minor (*Mondschein*) sonata op. 27 No. II, which belongs to this period. The direct incentive to its composition was Seume's poem, *die Beterin* in which he gives us a description of a daughter praying for her noble father, who has been condemned to death. But in this painful struggle with self, we also hear the storm of passion, in words as well as in tones. Beethoven's life at this time was one of sorrow. He writes: "I can say that I am living a miserable life. I have more than once execrated my existence. But if possible I shall bid defiance to fate, although there will be, I know, moments in my life when I shall be God's most unhappy creature." The thunders of power may be heard in the finale of that sonata. When it was published, the following year, its dedication ran: *Alla damigella contessa Giulietta Guicciardi.* The celebrated Giulietta! Her friendship was, indeed, a cheering ray of sunshine in Beethoven's "wretched life" at this time. As he writes himself in the fall of the year 1801:

> "My life is somewhat pleasanter now. I move about among men more than I used to. I am indebted for this change for the better to a lovely, charming girl who loves me and is loved by me. For two years now I have had once more some moments of happiness, and for the first time in my life I feel that marriage might make one happy. Unfortunately, she does not belong to my social circle. But if I cannot get married at the present time, I shall have to mix more among men."

The family of the imperial counsellor, Count Guicciardi, originally from Modena, was one of the families of the higher class with whom Beethoven had formed an intimate acquaintance through his art. Guicciardi's wife belonged to the Hungarian family of the Brunswicks, who were likewise very friendly to Beethoven. We shall yet have something to say of the Countess Theresa Brunswick, for whom and whose sister, the charming Countess Deym, the variations for four hands on *Ich denke dein*, were written in 1800. Countess Giulietta was in her sixteenth year, and as good as betrothed to Count Gallenberg, a musician and composer of ballet music. He was, however, in such pecuniary straits that Beethoven had, on one occasion, to come to his assistance through a friend. The young girl did not give any serious thought to a union with the Count, although he belonged to her own social circle. The attractions of a genuine love had more charms for her. This same true, genuine love possessed Beethoven's soul. He writes to his friend Wegeler:

> "I feel that my youth is only now beginning. Was I not always a sickly man? But, for a time, my physical strength has been increasing more than ever before, and the same is true of my mental power. With every succeeding day I approach nearer to the goal which I feel, but cannot describe. Thus only can I live. No rest I know of no repose but sleep, and it sorely pains me that I have now to allot more time to sleep than was once necessary. Let me be only half freed from my trouble and then, a perfectly mature man, I shall come to you and renew our old friendship. You must see me as happy as it is given me to be here below. You must not see me unhappy; that is more than I could bear. I shall struggle manfully with fate, and be sure, it will not overcome me entirely. O, how beautiful it would be to live life over a thousand times! But I am not made for a quiet life."

To this, Beethoven's elasticity of soul, which lifted him to the height of joy and of intellectual delight, we are indebted for those works of his which are models of poetic creation. What became of the traditional form of the sonata after Beethoven began to tell in song the meaning of joy and pain and of their wonderful admixture, as he did in the sonata op. 31, No. II, the first movement of which looks as if thrown off with a single stroke of the pen? There are the thoughtful questionings of fate in the opening chord; the jubilant, tempestuous enjoyment of pleasure; the expression of woe, more terrible in anticipation than realization, when misery wrings a cry of pain from him, and he breaks out in recitative—a form of art never before coupled with an instrument, but which is here more eloquent than words. Sorrow, joy and genius have now transformed the mere musician into the artist and the poet. Beethoven, as the master of the intellectual world of tones, began his career with this sonata in D minor. From this time forward, his every piece is a psychological picture of life. The form of the sonata had now fully developed the intellectual germ which in it lay. It is no longer mere form, but a finite vessel holding an infinite intellectual treasure as its contents. Even the separate parts of it, although retained as usual, are henceforth only phases and stages of the development of that intellectual treasure. They are acts of a drama played in the recesses of a human soul—in the soul of a man who is forced to taste, while still he laughs in his melancholy, the tragic contents of the cup of human life during every moment of his existence. For thus it was now with Beethoven. The deepest sorrow endows him with untrammeled serenity of mind. Darkness becomes to him the parent of a higher light. A humor that weeps through its smiles is henceforth his.

On this sonata followed a symphony with the real Beethoven flavor, the second symphony (op. 36). It had its origin in the "sublime feeling " which "animated" him in the beautiful summer days of 1802; as had also the brilliant *Kreutzer Sonata* (op. 47). This summer of 1802 is a memorable one in Beethoven's life. It brought with it the severest trials of his courage as a man. These trials transformed him into a hero, and were the incentives to the composition of the *Eroica*. To this period belongs the so-called "Heiligenstadt Will," which discloses to us the inmost depths of Beethoven's soul.

His physician had ordered him in October, 1802, to the village of Heiligenstadt, near Vienna, in a condition of the utmost hopelessness. Beethoven thought that death was not far off, and, anxious to justify himself before posterity, he wrote from that place:

"O, you men, who think or say that I am malignant, obstinate or misanthropic, what an injustice you do me! You know not the secret cause of what you think you see. From childhood up, my heart and mind have been bent upon the accomplishment of great deeds; I was ever moved thereto by the feeling of benevolence. To accomplish such deeds I was always disposed. But consider that for six—yes, six whole years, I have been in a most unfortunate condition—a condition which has been made worse by the stupidity of my physicians; that my hopes, from year to year, of being cured have been disappointed, and that at last there lies before me the prospect of permanent ill. Born with an active and even fiery temperament, a lover of the distractions of society, I had to live in a state of isolation from all men. How humbled I felt when a person standing near me could hear a flute that was playing in the distance, while I could hear nothing! Experiences like this brought me to the very verge of despair, and I came very near ending my own life. Art alone held me back. It seemed to me impossible that I should leave the world until I had accomplished all for which I felt myself so well fitted. O God, thou seest my heart. Thou seest that it harbors beneficence and love for human kind. O you men, when you read this, remember that you have wronged me, and let the unfortunate rejoice to find one of their number who, spite of the obstacles put in his way by nature, did all in his power to be admitted into the ranks of artists and men worthy of the name."

And now, too, we find in his music the first traces of such appeals to the Godhead. The text of the six songs of Gellert, op. 48, which appeared in 1803, are of a religious nature. But, in the domain of religion, our artist had not yet risen to his full height. He is still preponderantly the musician of life, force and of the brilliant play of the intellect; and his compositions are still preeminently works of art and of the fancy. The *Eroica* (op. 55), which was finished in 1803, possessed these characteristics in the highest sense of the word. And now we may understand what he felt himself, as he said in his "Will," fitted to accomplish, as well as the mysterious conversation he had in 1823, with his amanuensis, Schindler, in which he speaks of this period of his life, and of Giulietta, who had now long been the Countess Gallenberg, and who had, a short time before, returned from Naples, where her husband had acted as director of the theater for years. The conversation in question begins thus: It was held in the French language:

Beethoven—"She was mine before she was her husband's or Italy's, and she paid me a visit, bathed in tears; but I despised her."

Schindler—"By Hercules!"

Beethoven—"If I had parted in that way with my strength, as well as my life, what would have remained to me for nobler and better things?"

One of Beethoven's three primary music teachers, Christian Gottlob (or Gottlieb) Neefe (1748-1798). (Image/caption by the editor.)

Beethoven had said of himself that he had something to do in the world besides marrying. His ideal was not to live in such cramped circumstances. He knew of "nobler and better things." Yet it seems that he offered his hand to the "lovely, charming girl" in this year 1803, when he began to have a prospect of permanently bettering his condition, and that Giulietta was not disinclined to marry him. But family considerations prevented the decisive step; and she was married in the fall of the same year to Count Gallenberg. "Despising " her—whether rightly or wrongly we have no means of determining, but we do know that she was not happy—Beethoven turned to the performance of the great tasks for which he felt himself fitted.

Our artist's life, like that of a thousand others, thus proves the truth of the old saying: the course of true love never did run smooth. In his earlier biographies this episode has been treated as a great and even tragic event, because that remarkable letter to his "immortal love," of which we shall yet have occasion to speak, was erroneously supposed to be addressed to Countess Guicciardi and to refer to this circumstance in his life. But although no more than an episode, Beethoven could here have mastered his feelings only by the full consciousness he now possessed of the duty he owed to his genius. As Liszt says, *le genie oblige*, and Beethoven felt that it was a duty genius owed to mankind to sacrifice mere ambition and even the heartfelt happiness that is born of love. The day before Guilietta's wedding, he wrote to Macco, the painter: "You paint, and I shall compose music. In this way, we shall be immortal; yes, perhaps live forever." And that our artist had some right to lay claim to such immortality is proved not only by his sonatas, which are little poems in themselves, by his songs and quartets, but by mighty and memorable works which reflect the world-soul. He was working on that grand creation, the *Eroica*. This sacrifice of his feelings may have been, and most likely was, forced upon him by the accident of the uncertainty of his position in life, but that it was not made without a struggle is manifest from his expression of contempt for Giulietta—*mais je la meprisais* but still more from the ideal of the value of faithful love which now became rooted in his soul, and which we see reflected in the *Fidelio*, that immediately followed the *Eroica*, and which presents us with the most beautiful of all female characters. In its composition, we find united that warmth of heart and that intellectual in sight so peculiarly Beethoven's own, and which he so beautifully embodied in his art. On the golden background of his enthusiasm for "nobler and better things," the sweet face of Leonore stands out in bold relief as the perfect type of human beauty.

Beethoven borrowed the tones of the *Eroica* from the elevating nature of humanitarian ideas transferred to the region of public life. The hero enters, touching with giant hands the foundations of human existence, which he wants to ameliorate by renewing them. And, indeed, the First Consul of the French Republic might very well suggest to him, at the beginning of this century, how heroes act, the jubilation with which nations greet them, how great existing institutions oppose their progress, and, finally, overthrow them in their might. The first movement of the *Eroica* describes the most varied events in the life of such a hero with a fullness of episode almost destructive of its form. In its climax, the real work of the hero is seen; the old order of things is heard crumbling and falling to pieces in its powerful and terrific syncopations and dissonant chords, to make place for a new existence, one more worthy of human beings. But, at the close of the movement, the victorious hero exultingly yokes the new order of things to his chariot. This is history, the world's history in tones; and, for its sake, we may for the moment shroud the dearest longings of the heart in the dark robes of resignation.

Beethoven's fancy as an artist fully comprehended the genius of liberty, at this time newly born into the world, and a new factor in the history of mankind. He understood, too, the tragic fate of all heroes—that they are destined, like all other mortals, to fall, and, though God-commissioned, to die, that their works may live and prosper. Bonaparte's history also suggested the rhythm of the sublime and solemn step of the funeral march; for, since the days of Caesar and Alexander, no man had stepped as did he through the spaces of the existing order of things. But Beethoven's poetic fancy soared even now far beyond the reality that surrounded him. As early as 1802, he wrote to the music dealers in Leipzig, now so well known as the publishers of the *Edition Peters*: "Away with you all, gentlemen! To propose to me to write such a sonata! That might have done in the time when the Revolution was at fever heat, but now that everything has returned to the old beaten path, that Bonaparte has concluded a concordat with the Pope, to write such a sonata—away with you!" It is not Napoleon, therefore, who is here interred. It is not Napoleon for whom mankind weeps in the tones of this funeral march. It is the ever-living, ever-awakening hero of humanity, the genius of our race, that is solemnly borne to the grave to the rhythm of this wonderful march—a march which has in it something of the tragic pathos of a Shakespeare or an Aeschylus. Beethoven in this march became a tragic writer of purely instrumental music, and gave evidence of that quality of soul which made him indifferent to "the slings and arrows of outrageous fortune."

The two last movements of the work do not convey so powerful an idea of heroic action. Was it that his powers of imagination flagged, or that the change in Napoleon's career made him disgusted with the hero? We know that when, in the spring of 1804, the copy of the symphony was finished—the title, proudly and characteristically enough bearing only two names, "Buonaparte" at the top and "Luigi van Beethoven" at the bottom—and Beethoven heard of Napoleon's elevation, he said: "Can it be that he is no more than an ordinary man? Now he, like others, will trample all human rights under foot, serve only his ambition and become a tyrant." He tore the title page in two, threw the work on the floor and did not again look at it for a long time. When it appeared in 1806, it was under the name of the *Sinfonia Eroica*, "composed to celebrate the memory of a great man." It was dedicated to Prince Lobkowitz, who purchased it and caused it to be performed before Prince Louis Ferdinand, in the fall of 1804. The Prince was so delighted with it that he had it played three times the same evening in immediate succession, which was a very great satisfaction to Beethoven.

Beethoven in 1801, age 31. (Image/caption by the editor.)

There is a oneness of spirit in this instrumental fresco-painting of a hero who strives and suffers for the sake of what is most precious to man, and in Beethoven's only opera, the *Fidelio*, which made the latter the natural successor of the *Eroica*. Florestan dared "boldly to tell the truth," and this, his entering the lists for right and freedom, incites his faithful wife, Leonore, to a truly heroic deed. Disguised in male attire, she enters the prison, and, just in the nick of time, casts herself between her beloved husband and his murderer. Her cry—which has in it much of the heroism of death—"kill first his wife," is a bit of history showing the enthusiasm of the ideally great, as it is also the most intense dramatic representation, in tones, of the full energy of a woman's love.

In a letter to Amenda, in 1801, he wrote: "I have composed music of every description, except operas and church music." But even, a short time before this, he had something to do with the theater. He had written the ballet *Prometheus*, which represents in a sense, the history of the creation of man in choregraphic pictures. The success of this work determined Schikaneder, well known to the readers of the life of Mozart, and who, at this time, had the direction of the newly-built theater in Vienna, to engage Beethoven at a large annual stipend. When this man, Schikaneder, in the same spring of 1803, saw that the oratorio *Christus am Oelberg* ("Christ on the Mount of Olives") met with good success, although more theatrical than spiritual in its character, he commissioned him to write an opera also. The subject was, probably, *Alexander*—a very suitable one, considering Beethoven's own heroic style, and his feeling at the time. But nothing came of it. There can be no doubt, however, that a piece which he had sketched and intended to make a part of it, the duet, *O Namenlose Freude* ("O Nameless Joy"), was afterwards embodied in the *Fidelio*. Beethoven had received a commission to write the latter from Baron von Braun, who had taken charge of the theater in Vienna, in the year 1804.

At this time, both the Abbe Vogler and Cherubini were writing for the Viennese. The compositions of the latter met with great success, and made a powerful impression on Beethoven. In these men he met with foes worthy of his steel, and inducements great enough to lead him to do his very best. His severe heart trials and consequent disappointment had taught him how lonely he was in the world. Breuning wrote of him in 1804: "You have no idea, my dear Wegeler, how indescribable, and, I might say, horrible an impression his partial loss of hearing has made on him. . . . What must be the feelings of one with such a violent temper, to meet with such a misfortune! And then his reserve, and his distrust frequently of his best friend!" A subject like that of the *Fidelio* must, of itself, have taken strong hold of a man like Beethoven, because of the powerful scene in which Leonore holds her mortal enemy, Pizarro, spell-bound, with the pistol in her hand. What must have most affected him here, however, was the ideal background of suffering for truth and freedom—for Pizarro was a tyrant—and the fact that a woman had the power that comes of genuine fidelity to avert every danger from her beloved husband, even at the risk of her own life. And Beethoven endowed the work with his exalted and almost transfigured background of feeling, by means of his music, which here depicts the constitution of his own nature, and his whole intellectual build. He accurately hits the decisive climax of the conflict, and gives to the principal actors so much of real personal character, that we cannot fail to recognize them, and to understand their action from their inner feelings. This, in connection with a very powerful declamation, is the continuation of the dramatic characteristics which we greet in the *Fidelio*. The development of the operatic form as such is not further carried on in this work. In his pure instrumental music, even more than in the *Fidelio*, Beethoven has given form to the language of the soul and to the great hidden springs of action of the world and human nature.

A period may come when stricter demands may be made on dramatic art, and when, as a consequence, this work may not have as much charm as it has for us, because of its fragmentary character. But be this as it may, in some of its details it will always appeal irresistibly to the finest feeling. We find in it passages like those in Beethoven's improvisation which never failed to draw from his hearers tears of real happiness. The greater part of this language was, like Mozart's Cantilene, rich in soul. Yet melodies like *Komm*

Hoffnung, lass den letzen Schein, In des Lebens Fruehlingstagen and *O namen, namenlose Freude*, are of such a character that "humanity will never forget them." Like the Holy Grail, they furnish food and light at the same time, and, like certain forces, produce a greater yield in proportion as greater demands are made upon them. We frequently find in it expressions that are simply inimitable, and when this work is contemplated we see that it bears evidence of a profundity of soul and of a development of mind which separate—*toto coelo*—Beethoven from his predecessors, Mozart not excepted. Whole pieces in it are full of the deepest and warmest dramatic life, made up of the web and woof of the human soul itself. Such, for instance, are *Wir mussen gleich zu Werke schreiten*, the chorus of prisoners, the picture of Florestan's dungeon, the digging of the grave, and above all the thrilling *Toed't erst sein Weib!* ("kill first his wife"). But the center of all is, as may be seen from the innumerable and most refined traits of the music, Leonore, the pattern of heroic fidelity. Her character stirred Beethoven to the very depths of his soul, for her power of hope and her devotion to freedom were his own. The work itself was to be called *Leonore*, as, indeed, the first piano-score was called in 1810.

This work has a meaning in the life of our artist himself, greater, almost, than its importance as a work of art.

The work required, for its completion, only the spring and summer of the year 1805. The sketches of it show how carefully the file was used on its every part. Only the fire of enthusiastic devotion was able to smelt the ore of the separate arias, duets and terzettoes which make up the matter of the whole; but this it could not do here fully enough to produce that natural flow which dramatic taste even now demanded. Moreover, the storm of war broke upon Vienna and deprived Beethoven's hearers of even the calm of devotion. The result was that only the prima donna Milder-Hauptmann satisfied the public in the character of Leonore. Besides, Beethoven, as a composer of purely instrumental music, had not paid sufficient attention to the demands of the human

Archduke Rudolph of Austria (1788-1831). (Image/caption by the editor.)

voice. On the 13th of October, 1805, Napoleon entered Vienna; and after the 20th the *Fidelio* was repeated three times; not, however, before the art lovers of Vienna, but before an audience composed of French officers. It was received with little applause, and after the first performance the house remained empty. Beethoven withdrew the work. But even the critics missed in it at this time "that certain splendor of originality characteristic of Beethoven's works."

Our artist's friends now gathered about him to induce him to make some abbreviations in the opera. This was at the house of Lichnowsky. Beethoven was never before seen so much excited, and were it not for the prayers and entreaties of the gentle and tender Princess Christiane, he would certainly have agreed to nothing. He consented at last to drop a few numbers, but it took six full hours to induce him to do even this. It is easy to explain this fact: the work was the pet child of his brain. Breuning now re-arranged the libretto. He made the acting more vivacious and Beethoven shortened the several pieces still more. The work proved more acceptable to the public, but Beethoven thought himself surrounded by a network of intrigue, and, as he had agreed only for a share in the profits, he once more withdrew the work. We hear no more of it until 1814. We shall see what effect its production had when we reach that date in Beethoven's life.

But this re-arrangement led to a new overture and to a new poetical expression of the subject, to the great *Leonoren-Overture*, known as No. 3, but which is properly No. 2. Beethoven, in this overture, lets us hear, as if in the voices of thousands, the depth of pain in Florestan's dungeon; the glance of hope that flashes across his mind when he thinks of his Leonore; the struggle of love with native fear in the heart of the woman; her daring risk of her own life for her beloved husband, and in the signal of trumpets, the coming of her rescuer; the calm joy of the unutterably happy husband, as well as the boisterous, stormy joy of the prisoners, all of whom get their liberty with this one slave; and, last of all, the loudest song of praise of freedom and happiness. The symphonic poem, *Leonore*, as a whole, far surpasses the dramatic work itself. Together with the *Eroica*, it is the second monumental work of Beethoven's genius in this early period of his musical creations, and proves him a matured master in his art.

The proud path thus entered on, he never left.

Besides the works already mentioned, we may, for the sake of completeness, mention the following likewise: The *Opferlied* (1ˢᵗ arrangement), *Seufzen eines Unbeliebten*, variations *quant'e piu bello*, about 1795; variations to *Nel cor piu* and minuet *a la Vigano* which appeared in 1796; sonata op. 49, I, about 1796; sonata for four hands op. 6, the rondo op. 51, I, and variations to a Russian dance, in 1797; variations to a Swiss song and *Mich brennt*, 1798; *Gretels Warnung*, *La partenza*, composed in 1798; variations to the *La stessa*, *Kind willst du* and *Taendeln und Scherzen*, which appeared in 1799; sonata op. 49, I, composed in 1799; variations in G major, composed in 1800, serenade op. 25; rondo, op. 51, I; variations, *Bei Maennern*, which appeared in 1802; terzetto op. 116, sonatas for violin, op. 30, variations op. 34 and 35, composed in 1802; *Glueck der Freundschaft*, op. 88 and *Zaertliche Liebe* which appeared in 1803; trio variations op. 44 and romance for the violin, op. 40, composed in 1803; three marches op. 45, variations to "Rule Britannia," and the *Wachtelschlag*, 1804; sonata op. 53, together with the *andante* in F major, originally belonging to it, the *triple concerto* op. 56, and the sonata op. 57, begun in 1804, *Andie Hoffnung*, op. 32 and trio op. 38, which appeared in 1805; fourth concerto op. 58, composed in 1805; trio op. 36, sonata op. 34, which appeared in 1806; *Empfindungen bei Lydiens Untreue* belonging probably to 1806.

CHAPTER III

BEETHOVEN'S HEILEGENSTADT WILL, written in the year 1802, closed with this painful appeal: "O thou, Providence, let one day more of joy dawn on me. How long have I been a stranger to the heartfelt echo of true happiness! When, when, O God, can I feel it once more in the temple of nature and of man. Never? No! O, that were too hard!" Our artist's thoughts were thus directed into channels which carried him far from the scenes immediately surrounding him into regions of a higher existence—of an existence which he soon described so exquisitely in the language of music. The *Pastorale* which celebrates this "Temple of nature" was originally designated as No. 5, and was, therefore, intended to be completed before the symphony in

C minor. But it would seem that Beethoven had to go through many an internal conflict, the result of his great depression of spirits, before he could acquire the calmness of mind necessary to form a proper conception of the "Peace of God in Nature," and to give it proper form and expression in art.

Breuning wrote, on the 2nd of June, 1806, that the intrigues about the *Fidelio* were all the more disagreeable to Beethoven because the fact that it had not been performed reduced him to some pecuniary straits, and that it would take all the longer time for him to recover, as the treatment he had received deprived him of a great deal of his love for his work. Yet the first of the quartets, op. 59, bears the memorandum: "Begun on the 26th of May, 1806;" and the fourth symphony (op. 60), as well as the violin concerto (op. 61), also belong to this year. In the meantime op. 56, which had been begun some time previous, the triple concerto, op. 57, called the *Apassionata*, and op. 58, the fourth concerto, were all either continued or finished. What wealth there is here—in the number of compositions, in their magnitude and in their contents! The three quartets are dedicated to Count Rasumowsky, who had given Beethoven

Sketch of Beethoven.
(Image/caption by the editor.)

the commission to write them, and who had furnished the Russian melodies on which they are based. How well the *adagio* of the second of them points us to that higher region in which Beethoven now felt himself more and more at home. He himself told Czerny that that *adagio* suggested itself to him one night, when he was contemplating the starry heavens, and thinking of the harmony of the spheres. In the serene calmness of these vanishing tones, we see the revolution of the stars mirrored in all its grandeur. Here all pain seems lightened, all passion stilled. Yet how both had raged even

in the *Apassionata*, the draft of which is to be found immediately following that of the *Fidelio*. The *Apassionata* is written in his heartblood. Its tones are cries of excitement the most painful. It was finished in the summer, and dedicated to Count Franz Brunswick. An oil painting of the count's sister, Countess Theresa, was found among Beethoven's effects, after his death. It bore the superscription: "To the rare genius, the great artist, the good man. From T. B." It is supposed that the letter to his "immortal love," already referred to, was addressed to her—and it is truly a letter which gives us a pen-picture of Beethoven's condition of mind at that time, and which affords an idea of the "gigantic sweep of his ideas." It was found after his death, together with other important papers, in an old chest, and is dated on July 6, from a watering place in Hungary. It is rightly supposed to have been written in the year 1806, in which Beethoven paid a visit to the Brunswicks. But, be this as it may, it gives evidence of intense feeling, and shows that Beethoven now dwelt on that sublime height on which all earthly desires are silent. It seems also to lead us over to the understanding and appreciation of Beethoven's subsequent creations, which henceforth gain an ideal character not of this earth. We can here touch only on the principal points in these letters.

"My angel, my all, my other self." Thus does he begin it on the 6th of July, in the morning. He proceeds:

"Only a few words today, and those in lead-pencil, and that your own pencil, dear. Nothing can be settled about my dwelling until tomorrow. What a wretched loss of time for such trifles! Why this deep affliction where necessity speaks? How can our love continue to exist except through sacrifice, except by limitation of our desires? Can you change the fact that you are not entirely mine nor I entirely yours? Look out on the beauties of nature, and resign yourself to what must be. Love asks everything, and rightly so. It does in my case. It does in your case. But you forget too easily that I have to live for you as well as for myself. Were we entirely one, you would feel the pain there is in this as little as I. . . . We shall, I trust, soon meet. . . . . I cannot tell you to-day what reflections I have made upon my life, during the past forty-eight hours. Were our hearts always close to one another, I am sure I should make no such reflections. My heart is too full to tell you much. There are moments when I find that language is nothing at all. Cheer up; be my faithful, my only pet, my all, as I am all yours. The gods must direct the rest in our lives. Thy faithful Ludwig."

But, on the same dainty little piece of note paper, he continues, for the mail had already left:

"You suffer, dearest creature. Wherever I am, you are with me. I must try to so arrange it that our life may be one. But what, what a life to be thus without you! I am pursued by the kindness of men which I do not intend to earn, and yet, which I really do earn. That a man should humble himself before his fellow man, pains me; and when I consider myself as a part of the universe, what am I, and who is He they call the Most High? And yet here, again, we find the divine in that which is human. . . . No matter how great your love for me, my love for you is greater still. Never hide yourself from me. Good night! Being an invalid, I must go to sleep. Alas, that I should be so near and yet so far from you. Is not our love a real firmament of heaven? And is it not as firm as the foundation of the heavens?"

He takes up the same piece of paper once more:

"Good morning, this 7th of July! Even before I rise my thoughts fly to you, dear—to you, immortal love, now joyfully, now sadly, waiting to see whether the fates will hear our prayer. If I shall live at all, it must be with you. I am resolved to wander about far away from you, until the time comes when I may fly into your arms, and say that I belong to you; until I may send my soul absolved by you, dear, into the land of spirits. Yes, unfortunately it must be so. You will be all the more composed, since you know how faithful I am to you. Another can never possess my heart—never! Why, O God, must a man be so widely separated from the object of his love? And yet the life I now live in Vienna is so wretched! Your love makes me, at once, the happiest and the most unfortunate of men. At my present age, there should be some uniformity in my life; but is such a thing possible in my present circumstances? Be patient. Only by the patient contemplation of our existence can we gain our object and live united.

Be patient! Love me! How I longed and wept for you today and yesterday; you, my life, my all! Farewell; love me ever, never forget the most faithful heart of thy beloved Ludwig. I am ever thine and thou forever mine."

How completely like Beethoven! It was during this very summer that he completed the *Apassionata*, which he always considered the greatest of his sonatas, at the home of the Brunswicks. Can it be said that its language is in anything greater than the language of this letter? He seems at this time to be nearly always possessed by a feeling of melancholy. But for this very reason he took refuge more than ever in music. It was, indeed, a real sanctuary to him, and he refused to open that sanctuary to the eyes of strangers, and, least of all, to the eyes of enemies. This he very plainly proved to Prince Lichnowsky during the fall. Beethoven had left Hungary and was spending some time in Silesia with the prince. The latter desired him to play for some French officers who were quartered in his castle. A violent scene immediately ensued. After it was over, Beethoven left the castle. He

A painting of Beethoven in the year 1804, age 34. (Image/caption by the editor.)

refused to go back with the prince who had followed him, but repaired, post haste, back to Vienna, in which city the prince's bust was broken to pieces as an expiatory sacrifice. It was not long, however, before the old friendship of the two was reestablished.

In the quartet sketches of this year, we find the words: "Just as you can cast yourself here into the whirl of society, it is possible to write operas spite of all social impediments. Let the fact that you do not hear be a mystery no longer, even in your music." This "whirl of society" introduces us to some new acquaintances. Count Rasumowsky held very brilliant soirées, at which the amiable and charming wife of his librarian, Marie Bigot, performed some of Beethoven's works in an exquisite manner. The playing of the elegant and handsome Countess Marie Erdoedy, whom Beethoven himself called his "father confessor," was not inferior to that of Madame Bigot. Other patrons of the musical art were Madame Dorothea von Ertmann, a charming Frankfort lady, and the Malfattis, one of whom was Beethoven's physician. The home of Streicher, who had married Nanette Stein, daughter of the Augsbury piano-maker, described in Mozart's letter of 1777 in so droll a manner, was the rendezvous of lovers of music. Nor must we forget to mention Prince Lobkowitz and the Emperor's youngest brother, the Archduke Rudolph, Beethoven's distinguished pupil, who, as our artist himself admitted, understood music thoroughly.

The chief value, however, of the works quoted above, is that they inform us how Beethoven, spite of his experience with the *Fidelio*, was thinking very seriously of the writing of "operas." If successful here, his fortune was made, and there was nothing then to hinder the crowning of his love by marriage. There now seemed to be a very good prospect of that success, for, in the year 1807, the two court-theaters passed into the hands of a company of noblemen, with Lobkowitz at their head. Lobkowitz immediately called upon Beethoven to act as composer for the Court-theater. Our artist accepted the position, and bound himself to write at least one great opera and operetta each year, and to supply whatever other music might be needed. A feeling of inexhaustible power must have inspired him at this time, when he was actuated by the tenderest love, with the utmost confidence in self. A forcible proof of this is the overture which he then wrote to Collins's *Coriolanus*. But the gentlemen did not accede to his wishes; they did not want to trust him as composer of instrumental music in this point; and thus Beethoven, although not particularly pleased by the action of his princely friends, was, fortunately for himself and for us, retained in the field of labor most in harmony with his disposition.

"If it be true that genuine strength and a fullness of deep feeling characterize the Germans, we must say that Beethoven was, above all, a German artist. In this, his most recent work, we cannot but admire the expressiveness and depth of his music, which so grandly painted the wild, perturbed mind of *Coriolanus*, and the sudden and terrible change in his fate, while it elicited the sublimest emotion." These lines are from an account of a concert given in the *Augarten* by Lichnowsky in the spring of 1807. But we have very reliable information that Beethoven was now engaged on the symphony in C minor and on the *Pastorale*. Thanks to Clementi, who was doing a large and thriving music business in London, and to his old friend Simrock, in Bonn, which was French at the time, he felt at his ease so far as money matters were concerned. He writes to Brunswick on the 11th of May, 1807: "I can now hope to be able, in a few years, to maintain the dignity of a real artist." And when, in the same letter, we read the farther passage, "Kiss your sister Theresa. Tell her that I fear that I shall become great without a monument, to which she has contributed," we can understand how love, fame and lofty intuition conspired to fit him for new and mighty exploits in art.

The next work published by Beethoven was the Mass in C, op. 86, which Esterhazy gave him a commission to write. But here Beethoven, even more than in opera, missed the spirit of his subject. The Mass bears witness to his intellect, and has all the charms of sound; but it is not a religious composition. When Beethoven himself wrote to Esterhazy, as he did at this time: "Shall I tell you that it is not without many misgivings that I shall send you the Mass, for I know you are accustomed to have the inimitable works of the great Haydn performed for you," he proves that he did not understand the real spirit of church music; for Haydn had, just as little as Beethoven, a true conception of what church music is. Haydn was now seventy-six years old, and Beethoven attended a performance of his *Creation* the following year, and, with a number of the distinguished nobility, received the celebrated guest at the door. The fame of the man whom he was thus called upon to honor, was a type of what his own was destined one day to be. And what his own fame would be, the production of the great works he had recently finished, must have enabled him to foresee. When the Mass was performed, in September, 1807, in Eisenstadt, our composer had a personal falling out—the result of a misunderstanding—with Mozart's pupil, Hummel; and one which was not made up for for some years. The prince had criticized Beethoven's Mass by asking the strange question: "But, my dear Beethoven, what have you been doing now?" Hummel could not help laughing at this strange mode of criticism. Beethoven supposed he was laughing at his work; and after this would have nothing more to do with the prince.

It was otherwise with the magnanimous, noble lover of art, Prince Lobkowitz, one of the principal grandees of Bohemia, and one of the principal patrons of the theater. To him Beethoven was indebted for the suggestion that the *Fidelio* should be performed in Prague. For the occasion, Beethoven wrote, in this year, 1807, the overture, op. 138, which is, therefore, to be accounted not the second, but the third *Leonore* overture. The performance of the *Fidelio*, however, did not take place until 1814, the same year in which it was performed in Vienna. In the following summer (1808), it was publicly announced that "the

First page of Beethoven's Sonata No. 3 in C Major, Opus 2, written for Joseph Hayden in 1795. (Image/caption by the editor.)

gifted Beethoven had conceived the idea to put Goethe's Faust to music, as soon as he could find any one to prepare it for the stage." The first part of Faust had appeared in 1807, as a "tragedy;" and, as we shall see, the poem made a deep impression on our artist. Long after, and even on his death-bed, it occupied his thoughts. But he had, even now, written some Faust music—the symphony in C minor. To it we now turn, for it is one of the greatest of Beethoven's creations.

We have seen how Beethoven himself once said: "Power is the moral code of men who distinguish themselves above others." And so we hear how one person described him as "power personified;" how another said of him that "a Jupiter occasionally looked out through his eyes;" and a third, that "his magnificent forehead was the seat of majestic, creative power." Spurred on by the opposition of "fate," that is, by what nature had denied him, we see this power appear in all its concentration and sublimity. The power which has created, and which preserves all things, has been called "will," and music, one of its immediate phenomena, while the other arts are only reflections of that will, and reflect only the things of the world. In the first movement of the symphony in C minor, we feel the presence of this power or personal will, to an extent greater than in any other work of art. It there appears in fullest action, in all its nobility. The symphony might not inappropriately have been called the Jupiter-symphony; for it is a veritable head of Jove, such as only a Phidias could have imagined. Melody has been described as the history of the will illuminated by reason, and the sonata-form of the symphony is just such kind of melody. And it is this fifth symphony of Beethoven's, which, more than any other, tells us the most secret history of that personal will, of all its strivings and motions. No type in any art, could have suggested a Siegfried to Richard Wagner. Here Beethoven's genius acts as force, as will, and as the conscious intelligence of the prototype of the Great Spirit. Yet when the work was performed in Paris, Hector Berlioz heard his teacher, Lessieur, say of it—and this, although he was deeply moved by it—"but such music should not be heard." "Don't be afraid," was the reply, "there will be little of that kind of music written." How correct was the insight of the gifted Frenchman! Siegfried's *Rheinfahrt*, in the *Goetterdaemmerung*, is music of "that kind."

But it is only the night of sorrow that gives birth to the concentration of power. It is only by great effort that this energy can be maintained. And as Coriolanus finely presses all the darts aimed at him by his mother into her own heart, in defying sacrifice, so we find, in the background of this holiest and most manly will, the consciousness of the variety and transitory character of all things. In his heart of hearts, Beethoven feels that fate has knocked at his door, only because in his following the dictates of force and action, he has sinned against nature, and that all will is only transitoriness and self-deception. The *adagio* expresses subjection to a higher will. The consciousness of this highest act of the will, to sacrifice one's self and yet to preserve one's freedom, gave birth to the song of jubilation in the *finale* which tells not of the joy and sorrow of one heart only; it lifts the freedom which has been praised and sought for into the higher region of moral will. Thus the symphony in C minor has a significance greater than any mere "work of art." Like the production of religious art, it is a representation of those secret forces which hold the world together.

The consciousness of this deeper, intimate dependence of all things on one another, is henceforth seen like a glimmer of light in the darkness which gathered around him, and it continues to beautify and transfigure his creations.

The *Pastorale* immediately followed the symphony in C minor. It gives expression to the peace of nature and to the fulfillment of the saying: "Look out on the beauties of nature and calm your soul by the contemplation of what must be." While the fourth symphony compared with the fifth, is a symphony and nothing more—even if it be Beethoven's—we plainly discover in this sixth, the poetic

Another key music teacher in Beethoven's early life, Johann Georg Albrechtsberger (1736-1800). (Image/caption by the editor.)

spirit, the pure feeling of God. The idea and character it illustrates constitutes in Beethoven's life the transition from the external beauty of nature to the comprehension of the eternal. Over it is written: "Recollections of country life," but also, "More an expression of feeling than a painting." "The Beethovens loved the Rhine," the young playmates of the boy Ludwig were wont to say, and he wrote himself to Wegeler: "Before me is the beautiful region in which I first saw the light as plainly and as beautiful as the moment I left you." On a leaf, written in his own hand, we find the words: "O the charm of the woods—who can express it?" But now that he was compelled to live a solitary life, nature became to him a mother, sister and sweetheart. He looked upon the wonders of nature as into living eyes; she calmed him who was naturally of such a stormy temperament, and to whom life had been unkind in so many ways. In the *Scene am Bach* ("Scene by the Brook"), the waters murmur peace to his soul; and the birds by the brooklet, in Heiligenstadt, where these two symphonies were finished, whisper joy. His *Lustige Zusammensein der Landleute*, infuses new courage into the heart, and when his *Gewitter und Sturm*, tells of the might of the Eternal, the shepherds express their joyful and grateful feelings in the words: *Herr wir danken dir*. The finale, like the *Chorphantasie* (op. 80), planned in 1800 but not finished until 1808, was intended to contain a chorus expressing in words the joyful and thankful feeling of the people. Beethoven's own personal experience is always expressed in his music. A more intimate acquaintance with nature gave it to him to find yet deeper expression for the feelings which it excites in our hearts, as its everlasting change enabled him to conceive the eternal and imperishable.

We now turn to a whole series of new and brilliant creations of our hero. It would seem as if his intercourse with the eternal in nature had given him new life.

During these years, Beethoven's intimacy with the Malfattis and their two charming daughters, was a great source of pleasure to him. His feelings towards them may be inferred from the following passages in his notes to his friend Gleichenstein. He writes: "I feel so well when I am with them that they seem able to heal the wounds which bad men have inflicted on my heart." . . . "I expect to find there in the *Wilden Mann* in the park, no wild men, but beautiful graces." And again: "My greetings, to all who are dear to you and to me. How gladly would I add—and to whom we are dear???? These points of interrogation are becoming, at least in me." Gleichenstein married the second daughter, Anna Malfatti, in 1811. To the young dark-eyed Theresa, who made her debut in society about this time, and whom he writes of as "volatile, taking everything in life lightly" but "with so much feeling for all that is beautiful and good, and a great talent for music," he sends a sonata, and recommends Goethe's Wilhelm Meister and Schlegel's translation of Shakespeare. We thus see that his intercourse with the family had that intellectual foundation which Beethoven could not dispense with, on anything. It would even seem as if, in his enthusiasm to put his strength to the test of new deeds, even his "eternal loved one" should fade from his view.

The cello-Sonata (op. 69) dedicated to his friend Gleichenstein immediately followed the *Pastorale*. The two magnificent trios dedicated to Countess Erdoedy, with whom he resided at this time, follow as op. 70. The first movement of the trio in D major is a brilliantly free play of mind and force, while the *adagio* suggests Faust lost in the deep contemplation of nature and its mysteries. The whole, on account of the mysterious awe expressed by this movement has been called by musicians the *Fledermaustrio*, i.e., the "bat-trio." The *Leonore* is numbered op. 72. It was published in 1810. Op. 73, the most beautiful of all concertos, was dedicated to the Archduke Rudolph. We have further, op. 74, the harp-quartet, dedicated to Prince Lobkonitz, and the fantasia for the piano, op. 77, to his friend Brunswick; lastly, the sonata in F sharp major, op. 78, very highly valued by Beethoven himself, dedicated to his sister Theresa. Verily "new acts" enough, and what glorious deeds!

This brings us to the year 1809, which witnessed a change for the better in Beethoven's pecuniary circumstances. He now received a permanent salary. On the 1st of November, 1808, he wrote to the Silesian Count, Oppersdorf,—whom he had visited in the fall of 1806, in company with Lichnowsky, and who gave him a commission to write a symphony, which the count, however, never received—as follows: "My circumstances are improving without the assistance of people who entertain their friends with blows. I have also been called to act as capellmeister to the King of Westphalia, and perhaps I may obey the call." The following December, Beethoven gave a great concert, the programme of which embraced the two new symphonies, parts of his Mass, the concerto in G minor, and the *Chorphantasie*. He himself improvised at the piano. The attention of people far and near was called anew to this great and grave master in music, whom the sensualist Jerome Bonaparte endeavored to attract to his Capua in Cassel, and they became anxious lest he might leave Vienna. Beethoven's friends bestirred themselves to keep him in Vienna, as did Beethoven himself to stay. This is very evident from the letters to Gleichenstein and Erdoedy. Three friends of his, to whom it was largely due that he wrote one of his greatest works, were instrumental in keeping him in Vienna. They were the Archduke Rudolph, Prince Lobkowitz and Prince Kinsky, to whose wife the six songs, op. 75, are dedicated. The sum guaranteed amounted to eight thousand marks. "You see, my dear good Gleichenstein," he writes, on the 18th of March, 1809, *a propos* of the "decree" which he had received on the 26th of February, from the hands of the archduke, and which imposed on him no duty but to remain in Vienna and Austria, "how honorable to me my stay here has become." He could not, however, have meant seriously what he added immediately after: "The title of imperial *capellmeister* will come to me also;" for what use had a man like the Emperor Franz for such an "innovator" at his court? The dedications of his works mentioned above were simply testimonials of gratitude for the friendship thus shown him.

He now planned an extensive journey, which was to embrace England, and even Spain. He writes to Gleichenstein: "Now you can help me get a wife. If you find a pretty one—one who may perhaps lend a sigh to my harmonies, do the courting for me. But she must be beautiful; I cannot love anything that is not beautiful; if I could I should fall in love with myself." The coming war interrupted all his plans. But, at the same time, it suggested to the imagination of our artist, that wonderful picture of the battle of forces, the seventh (A major) symphony (op. 92), which Richard Wagner has called the "apotheosis of the dance." Germany now first saw the picture of a genuinely national war. Napoleon appeared as Germany's hereditary foe, and the whole people, from the highest noble to the meanest peasant rose up, as one man, to fight the battle of freedom. The march is, after all, only the dance of war, and Beethoven gathered into one picture of instrumentation, the glad tramp of warlike hosts, the rhythm of trampling steeds, the waving of standards and the sound of trumpets, with a luminousness such as the world had never witnessed before. The poet needs only see the eddy created by a mill-wheel to paint the vapor and foam of

A letter written in Beethoven's hand. (Image/caption by the editor.)

Charybdis. In the case of Beethoven, this joy in the game of war was, as the character of Bonaparte, on another occasion, a stimulant to his imagination, which now painted a picture of the free play of force and of human existence from the material of recent historical events. And even in after years the timeliness of this work and the spirit which called it into existence were evident. And, as we shall soon see, it constituted the principal part in the musical celebration, when, in 1813, the real war of emancipation occurred and led to a most decided victory. Personally, Beethoven felt himself not inferior to the mighty conqueror in natural power, and, like Schiller, he clearly foresaw the awakening of the national genius which overthrew Napoleon. To this second-sight of the prophet, possessed by every genuine poet—to this sure presentiment of ultimate triumph—our artist owed it, that, even in the days of Germany's greatest ignominy and subjection he sang of the disenthrallment of the mind and of the jubilation of victory. Napoleon defeated the Austrians again. But as Beethoven first felt the weight and the power of resistance of Germany after the battles of Aspern and Wagram, he now depicted (after Napoleon had taken the Emperor's daughter to wife and seemed predestined to become the despot of all Europe), in the *scherzo* and *finale* of the seventh symphony, better than ever before, the jubilation of the victorious nation, with all its popular feasts and games. Yet, in the melancholy second part, with its monotonous beats on the *dominante*, we think we hear the gloomy rhythm of a funeral march. This exceedingly characteristic theme is found at the very beginning of a sketch-book of the year 1809.

Affairs were for a time in a very bad condition in Vienna and all Austria. The burthen of taxation was severely felt. Everything was at a standstill. When his beloved pupil, the Archduke Rudolph retreated from Vienna he wrote the *Lebewohl* of the sonata op. 81ᵃ; but its *finale* (*die Ankunft*) was not written until the 30th of January, 1810. The summer was a dreary one to Beethoven, and there was no demand for the exercise of his genius. Following Ph. E. Bach,

Kirnberger, Fux and Albrechtsberger he prepared the *Materiellen zum Generalbass* ("materials for thoroughbass") for his noble pupil. This work was subsequently but wrongly published under the name of *Beethoven's Studien*. On the 8th of September, a charity concert was given at which—to the disgrace of the period, be it said, for Napoleon had only just left Schoenbrunn—the *Eroica* was performed, Beethoven himself holding the baton. The rest of the summer he hoped to spend in some quiet corner in the country. He sojourned sometime with the Brunswicks in Hungary, and composed those works of his genius, op. 77 and 78. His genius, indeed, seems to have awakened to a new life during this fall of 1809. For the sketch-book of the seventh symphony (op. 92) contains sketches of the 8th (op. 93) also; and Beethoven contemplated giving another concert at Christmas, at which, of course, only new works could be performed. These sketches are followed by drafts for a new concerto. On these drafts we find the words: *Polonaise fuer Clavier allein, also Freude Schoener Goetterfunken*—"finish the overture" and "detached periods like princes are beggars, not the whole." He here takes up once more those ideas of his youth, but with a grander conception of their meaning. They constitute the intellectual germ of the *finale* of the ninth symphony. But the melody which he actually noted down was elaborated in 1814 into the overture op. 115 (*Zur Namensfeier*).

During this period of Germany's national awakening, the theaters had again turned their attention to Schiller's dramas. The effect of this was to revive Beethoven's youthful ideas. He now desired to give *Tell* a musical dress. He had already received a commission of this kind for the *Egmont*, and, on the occasion of his receiving it, he gave expression to a remarkable opinion. Said he to Ezerny: "Schiller's poems are exceedingly difficult to set to music. The composer must be able to rise high above the poet. But who can rise higher than Schiller? Goethe is much easier." And, indeed, his *Egmont* overture breathes a higher spirit and takes a loftier flight than Goethe's beautiful tragedy. The composition of this music led to his more intimate acquaintance with the poet. To this same year, 1810, belong the incomparable songs *Kennst du das Land*, and *Herz mein Herz*, in op. 75.

This year, 1810, brings us to a somewhat mysterious point in Beethoven's life, to his *Heirathspartie* (marriage speculation).

In the spring, he writes to his friend Zmeskall: "Do you recollect the condition I am in—the condition of Hercules before Queen Omphale? Farewell, and never again speak of me as the great man, for I never felt either the weakness or the strength of human nature as I do now." But writing to Wegeler on the second of May, he says: "For a couple of years I have ceased to lead a quiet and peaceful life. I was carried by force into the world's life. Yet I would be happy, perhaps one of the very happiest of men, were it not that the demon has taken up his abode in my ears. Had I not read somewhere that man should not voluntarily take leave of life while he is still able to do one good deed, I should long have departed hence, and by my own act. Life is very beautiful, but, in my case, it is poisoned forever." He asked for the certificate of his baptism, and this in a manner so urgent that it creates surprise. It was three months before the answer to the enigma was found, and Breuning wrote that he believed that Beethoven's engagement was broken off. But it continues a mystery, even to this day, who his choice was. It has been surmised that it was his "immortal loved one," or Theresa Brunswick. But we know nothing certain on this point. True, he had now acquired both fame and a position which raised him above all fear of want. But she was thirty-two years old, and he hard of hearing. In addition to this, there was, on his side, a relationship of the nature of which we shall yet have something to say. Her passion, if such there was on her part, must have been prudently concealed; and it is certainly remarkable that, from this time forward, her name is not mentioned by Beethoven. However, her niece, Countess Marie Brunswick, who is still living, expressly writes: "I never heard of any intimate relation nor of any love between them, while Beethoven's profound love for my father's

Beethoven circa 1808, 38 years old. (Image/caption by the editor.)

cousin, Countess Guicciardi, was a matter of frequent mention." But Giulietta had at this time long been Countess Gallenberg. The solution of this mystery, accordingly, belongs to the future.

On the other hand, we have a few notes to Gleichenstein, who married the younger Malfatti, the following year. In one of them we read: "You live on still, calm waters—in a safe harbor. You do not feel or should not feel the distress of the friend who is caught in the storm. What will people think of me in the planet Venus Urania? How can one judge of me who has never seen me? My pride is so humbled, that even without being ordered to do so, I would travel thither with thee." And, in the other: "The news I received from you cast me down again out of the regions of happiness. What is the use of saying that you would send me word when there was to be music again? Am I nothing more than a musician to you and to others? Nowhere but in my own bosom can I, find a resting-place. Externally, to myself there is none. No, friendship and feelings like it have only pain for me. Be it so, then. Poor Beethoven, there is no external happiness for you. You must create your own happiness. Only in the ideal world do you find friends." The sketch of that and Klaerchen's song *Freudvoll und leidvoll* were found in the possession of Theresa Malfatti. When Gleichenstein was engaged, the feelings of the man who had been so bitterly deceived overflowed. But how could the young girl of eighteen dare to do what the grave Countess would not venture? Theresa Brunswick died unmarried. Theresa Malfatti married, in 1817, one Herr von Drossdick. Nevertheless, Beethoven's intercourse with the family continued.

We next hear of his acquaintance with Bettina Brentano which led to his meeting Goethe in person. Her brother Francis had married a Miss Birkenstock, of Vienna. Beethoven had been long and well acquainted with the Birkenstock family. Bettina Brentano herself was betrothed to Achim von Arnim, and her deep love of music had inspired her with a genuine affection for Beethoven. One beautiful day in May, she, in the utmost simplicity of heart, went, in company with her married sister, Mrs. Savigny, to Beethoven and met with the very best reception. He sang for her *Kennst du das Land*, with a sharp and unpleasant voice. Her eyes sparkled. "Aha!" said Beethoven, "most men are touched by something good. But such men have not the artist's nature. Artists are fiery and do not weep." He escorted her home to Brentano's, and after this they met every day.

Bettina at this time sent Goethe an account of the impression made on her by Beethoven's appearance and conversation. Her charming letters are to be found in the Cotta *Beethovenbuch*. They show how exalted an idea Beethoven had of his own high calling. She writes: "He feels himself to be the founder of a new sensuous basis of the intellectual life of man. He begets the undreamt-of and the uncreated. What can such a man have to do with the world? Sunrise finds him at his blessed day's work, and at sunset he is as busy as at early morning. He forgets even his daily food. O! Goethe, no Emperor or King is as conscious of his power and of the fact that all power proceeds from him, as is this man Beethoven." And Goethe, who "loved to contemplate and fix in memory the picture of real genius," who well knew "that his intellect was even greater than his genius, and who frequently throws from himself a luminousness like that of lightning, so that we can scarcely tell, as we sit in the darkness, from what side the day may break," invited him to Carlsbad, whither he was wont to go every year.

The two remarkable letters to Bettina of the 11th of August, 1810, and the 10th of February, 1811, the autographs of which have since been found, show us how deeply the heart of our artist was stirred by love at this time. They are to be found in "Beethoven

Letters." A work of his composed about this time, the *Quartetto serioso*, op. 95, of October, 1810, throws some light on this love, and yet it rises far above the pain and the sorrow of the situation in which he found himself. Heavy thunders announce Vulcan at work; but in the *finale*, how Beethoven's giant mind frees itself from itself! The noble, powerful soaring Trio op. 97 dates from the spring of 1811, and, especially in the *adagio*, gives evidence of wonderful heartfelt bliss. But the fact that in this period no other compositions were written would go to show the influence of bitter experience. It may be, however, that the commission he received for the plays "The Ruins of Athens" and "King Stephen," took up the best portion of his time; and, besides, the two symphonies had to be finished. The song *An die Geliebte* also belongs to this year 1811, as well as the principal draft of op. 96, the charmingly coquettish sonata for the violin which was finished in 1812, on the occasion of the visit of the then celebrated violin player Rode to Vienna.

Beethoven's work on these two plays took up the summer of 1811, but they were not put upon the stage until the spring of 1812. At the same time, an opera was wanted for Vienna. It was the "Ruins of Babylon." He also received an invitation to Naples, where Count Gallenberg was director of the theater. We next find him traveling to Teplitz, a bathing place, where he formed a more intimate acquaintance with Varnhagen, Tiedge and Elise von der Recke. Amalie Sebald, a nut-brown maid of Berlin, twenty-five years of age, was stopping with Elise. Amalie had a charming voice, and was as remarkable for her intellectual endowments as for her beauty of physique. Beethoven, spite of his many disappointments, was greatly taken with her. Her picture is before us. Her eye betokens intellect and nobility of soul, and her mouth extreme loveliness. Beethoven subsequently wrote to Tiedge: "Press the Countess's hand for me very tenderly, but very respectfully. Give Amalie a right loving kiss, when no one is looking." He did not see Goethe on this occasion. He was at Teplitz again the following year, when his meeting—of which so much has been said and written—"with the most precious jewel of the German nation," as he called Goethe, when writing to Bettina, occurred. We can here give only the principal incidents of that event.

The Austrian imperial couple, their daughter, the Empress of France, the King of Saxony, the Duke of Saxe-Weimar, and a great many Princes were there. The company already in the place was joined by Goethe, the jurist Savigny and his brother-in-law, A. von Arnim, together with his charming wife, Bettina. Beethoven himself writes on the 12th of August, 1812, to his Archduke in Vienna: "I was in Goethe's company a great deal." And the poet, writing to Zelter, passes the following judgment on Beethoven:

> "I became acquainted with Beethoven in Teplitz. His wonderful talent astounded me. But, unfortunately, he is an utterly untamed character. He is not, indeed, wrong in finding the world detestable. Still, his finding it detestable does not make it any more enjoyable either to himself or to others. But he is very excusable and much to be pitied. His hearing is leaving him. He is by nature laconic, and this defect is making him doubly so."

The remarkable incident related in the third letter to Bettina, a letter which has been widely read and the authenticity of which has been much contested—for the original does not seem to be extant—Bettina herself describes in a letter to Pueckler-Muskau. Goethe, she says, who had received many marks of attention from the Princes present, was desirous of testifying his special devotion to the Empress, and in "solemn, unassuming expressions" signified to Beethoven that he should do the same. But Beethoven replied: "What! You must not do so. You must let them clearly understand what they possess in you; for if you do not, they will never find it out. I have taken quite a different course." And then he told how his Archduke once sent him word to wait, and how, instead of doing so, he went away. Princes might indeed, he said, decorate one with the insignia of an order, or make a man a court counsellor, but they could never make a Goethe or a Beethoven. To such men they

owed respect. The whole court now came in. Beethoven said to
Goethe: "Keep my arm; they must make way for us." But Goethe
left him and stood aside with his hat in his hand, while Beethoven,
with folded arms, went through the midst of them and only
touched his hat. The court party separated to make place for him,
and they had all a friendly greeting for our artist. He stood and
waited at the other end for Goethe, who bowed profoundly as the
court party passed him. Now Beethoven said: "I have waited for
you, because I honor and respect you, as you deserve, but you have
done them too much honor." Then, it is said, Beethoven ran to
them, and told them all that had happened.

That his behavior, on this occasion, was not by any means
dictated by any overestimation of himself, but by a deep human
feeling of equality—an equality which the artist finds it harder than
any one else to assert and acquire—the whole course of
Beethoven's life, as well as his intercourse
with people at this bathing place at
Teplitz, proves. He there found Miss
Sebald again. A series of very tender notes
written to her tells us of his heartfelt and
good understanding with this refined and
clever North German lady, who made
greater allowances for his natural
disposition than were wont to be made.
He writes in 1816: "I found one whom, I
am sure, I shall never possess." His
admission that, for five years—that is
from 1811,—he had known a lady to be

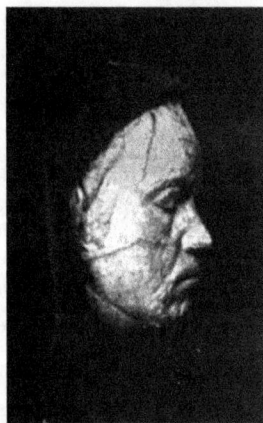

A cast of Beethoven's living
face in 1812, when he was 42
years old. (Image/caption by
the editor.)

united to whom he would have esteemed
it the greatest happiness he could have on
earth, was made in this same year. But, he
added, that was a happiness not to be thought of; union with her
was an impossibility, a chimera! And yet he closed with the words:
"It is still as it was the first day I saw her. I cannot dismiss the

thought of her from my mind." He did not know that Amalie Sebald had been the wife of a councillor of justice named Krause. Again did he give vent to his feeling in the songs *An die ferne Geliebte*—"to the distant loved one"—which bear the date; "in the month of April, 1816."

This was the last time that Beethoven seriously concerned himself about marriage. Fate would indeed have it that he should soon become a "father," but without a wife. Yet no matter what the personal wishes of our artist through the rest of his life may have been, or what the wants he felt, his eye was ever fixed on a lofty goal; and it was in the ideal world that he found his real friends. He finished the seventh symphony, and after it the eighth, in this fall of 1812. The coquettish *allegretto scherzando* of the latter was suggested by the Maelzl metronome invented a short time before, and the strange minuet with its proud step is a hit at the high court society whom Beethoven so solemnly warned that the times of the old regime, when the principle *l'etat c'est moi* obtained in society, were passed. These works are clearly expressive of the free and progressive spirit of a new and better age. It was the seventh symphony especially that, in the broadest sense, opened to Beethoven himself the hearts of that age. This symphony helped celebrate the newly-won peace established by the Congress of Vienna. Beethoven now entered a new stage of development, and rose to his full height as an artist and a man. Other works composed by Beethoven during this period are the following: 32 variations (1806–7); *In questa tomba* (1807); *sonatine* (op. 79); variations op. 76 and *Lied aus der Ferne* (composed 1809); *die laute Klage* (probably 1809; Sextett op. 8ᵇ. *Andenken, Sehnsucht* by Goethe, *der Liebende, der Jungling in der Fremde* (appeared in 1810); three songs by Goethe, op. 83 (composed in 1810); Scotch songs (commenced in 1810; four ariettes, op. 82, (appeared 1811); trio in one movement and three *equale* for four trombones, (composed in 1812) the latter of which was re-arranged as a dirge for Beethoven's burial.

CHAPTER IV

ESIGNATION, THE MOST absolute and heartfelt resignation to thy fate! Thou shouldst not live for thyself, but only for others. Henceforth there is no happiness for thee, but in thy art. O God, grant me strength to conquer myself. Nothing should now tie me to life." With this cry of the heart, taken *verbatim* from his diary of 1812, Beethoven consecrated himself to the noble task which after this he never lost sight of—of writing "for the honor of the Almighty, the Eternal, the Infinite."

The national bankruptcy of Austria did not leave Beethoven unaffected. It compelled him, besides, to come to the assistance of his sick brother, Karl. The first thing, therefore, that he felt called upon to undertake, in order to provide himself with the mere means of subsistence, was the public representation of his new compositions. It was not long before an occasion of an extraordinary kind offered, an occasion which lifted Beethoven's creations to the dignity of one of the motive powers of the national life of the period. The star of Napoleon's destiny was declining; and the gigantic struggle begun to bring about the overthrow of the tyrant of Europe, enlisted the sympathy and active participation of our artist.

"To abandon a great undertaking and to remain as I am! O, what a difference between the un-industrious life I pictured to myself so often! O, horrible circumstances which do not suppress my desire to be thrifty, but which keep one from being so. O, God! O, God! look down on thy unhappy Beethoven. Let this last no longer as it is." Thus did he write in May, 1813, in his diary. Madame Streicher, interested herself in him in his pecuniary embarrassment, which was so great that at one time, he did not have so much as a pair of boots to leave the house in. He writes: "I do not deserve to be in the condition I am—the most unfortunate of my life." The payments due him from Kinsky did not come, because of his sad death, and Prince Lobkowitz's love of music and the theater had greatly embarrassed him financially. Even the giving of a concert which he contemplated had to be abandoned in consequence of the bad times.

Beethoven in 1814, age 44. (Image/caption by the editor.)

The idea of a journey to London now took possession of him all the more strongly because of the straits to which he was reduced. This journey was, doubtless, the "great undertaking" referred to above. It is deserving of special mention here, because to it we are indebted for the ninth symphony.

Maelzl, the inventor of the metronome, had built a panharmonicum, and was anxious to make the journey to London in company with Beethoven. He had had the burning of Moscow set for his instrument; and he now wanted a musical representation of the next great event of the time—Wellington's victory at Vittoria. He suggested the idea to Beethoven. Beethoven's hatred of Napoleon and love of England induced him to adopt it, and this was the origin of the *Schlachtsymphonie* ("Battle-symphony") op. 91. For, in accordance with Maelzl's proposition, he elaborated what was at first a trumpeter's piece into an instrumental composition. It was performed before a large audience "for the benefit of the warriors made invalids in the battle of Hanau." And—, irony of fate!—a work which Beethoven himself declared to be a "piece of stupidity," took the Viennese by storm, and at a bound, made him very popular in Vienna.

It was performed on the 12th of December, 1813. The applause was unbounded. All the best artists of the city were with him. Salieri, Hummel, Moscheles, Schuppanzigh, Mayseder, and even strangers like Meyerbeer, assisted him. The Seventh Symphony was the ideal foundation of the entire production, for that symphony was the expression of the awakening of the heroic spirit of the nation. Anton Schindler, of whom we have already spoken more than once, and of whom we shall have more to say in the sequel, as Beethoven's companion, writes: "All hitherto dissenting voices, with the exception of a few professors of music, finally agreed that he was worthy of the laurel crown." He rightly calls the production of this piece one of the most important events in Beethoven's life; for now the portals of the temple of fame were opened wide to receive him; and if he had had nothing "nobler or better" than this to do in life, he certainly would never again feel the want of the good things of this world.

His next concern was to turn the occasion of the moment to advantage, to give some concerts with *Wellington's Victory*, and thus obtain leisure to work. Pieces from the "Ruins of Athens" also were played at these concerts. The success of one aria in particular from that composition suggested to one of the singers of the court-opera the idea of reviving the *Fidelio*. It then received the form in which we have it today. And what a hold the character of Leonore still had on our artist's soul, we learn from the account of the dramatic poet, Treitschke, who again tried to abridge the text. He had given expression to the last flash of life in the scene in Florestein's dungeon, in the words:

"Und spürich nicht linde, sanft säuselnde Luft,
  Und ist nicht mein Grab mir erhellet?
Und seh' wie ein Engel im rosigen Duft
  Sich tröstend zur Seite mir stellet,
Ein Engel, Leonoren, der Gatten so gleich,
Der führt mich zur Freiheit ins himmlische Reich."

"What I now tell you," he continues, "will never fade from my memory. Beethoven came to me in the evening. He read, ran up and down the room, murmured, growled, as he usually did instead of singing, and tore open the pianoforte. My wife had frequently begged him in vain to play. Today he placed the text before him and began playing wonderful melodies, which unfortunately no charm could preserve. The hour passed. Beethoven, however, continued his improvisation. Supper was served but he would allow no one to disturb him. It grew quite late. He then put his arms about me and hurried home. A few days after the piece was finished."

At this time he wrote to Brunswick: "My kingdom is in the air. My soul trills as the winds warble;" and to Treitschke: "In short I assure you, the opera will win the crown of martyrdom for me." Thus Leonore's sorrows and victory found expression a second time; for now the so called *Fidelio* overture (E major) was composed. At its performance on the 23rd of May, 1814, Beethoven was after the very first act, enthusiastically called for and enthusiastically greeted. The applause increased with every succeeding performance.

Beethoven was now one of the best known characters in Vienna. He had, even before this, given several concerts of his own, and at several others music composed by him had been

Another one of Beethoven's early music teachers, Franz Joseph Haydn (1732-1809). (Image/caption by the editor.)

performed. His picture by Letronne appeared at this time. "It is as natural as life," said Dr. Weissenbach. He had, on the 26th of September, received with his music of the *Fidelio*, the assemblage of monarchs who had come to attend the Congress of Vienna; and what was more natural than that he should now greet them with something new in the nature of festal music? He did this with the cantata, *der Glorreiche Augenblick* ("the Glorious Moment") op. 136. The production of it took place in the ever memorable Academy, on the 29th of November, 1814, when Beethoven, before a "parterre of kings," and what was more, before the educated of Europe, by the mere assistance of his art, helped celebrate the solemn moment which did away with oppression and tyranny and marked the beginning of a new and happier period. His audience was numbered by thousands, and "the respectful absence of all loud signs of applause gave the whole the character of worship. Every one seemed to feel that never again would there be such a moment in his life." This extract is from Schindler's account, yet, at certain places "the ecstasy of all present found expression in the loudest applause, applause which drowned the powerful accompaniment of the composer." The *Schlachtsymphonie* ("Battle-symphony") as well as the seventh symphony, contributed to the achievement of this victory. After it was over, he wrote to the archduke: "I am still exhausted by fatigue, vexation, pleasure and joy." But to get an idea of the overpowering impression made on him by those days, we must refer to his diary of the following spring, when all that he had then experienced took a definite form in his feelings and consciousness. He then writes:

"May all my life be sacrificed to the sublime. May it be a sanctuary of art. . . . Let me live, even if I have to have recourse to 'assistance,' and such means can be found. Let the ear apparatus be perfected if possible, and then travel! This you owe to man and the Almighty. Only thus can you develop what is locked up within you. The court of a prince, a little orchestra to write music for, and to produce it, for the honor of the Almighty, the Eternal, the Infinite. Thus may my last years pass away, and to future humanity. . . ."

He breaks off here as if he did not need to express an opinion on what he aimed at achieving and left after him as an inheritance. But the reputation which he had acquired is correctly described as "one of the greatest ever won by a musician." And now, more than ever before, he was the object of universal attention, especially at the brilliant entertainments given by the Russian ambassador, count Rasumowsky, to the monarchs present, on one of which occasions he was presented to them. The Empress of Russia wished to pay him a special "compliment." She did so at the palace of Archduke Rudolph, who thus helped celebrate the triumph of his honored teacher. At a court concert on the 25th of January, 1815, he accompanied the *Adelaide* for Florestan Wild himself; and Schindler closes his account of it with the words: "The great master recalled those days with much feeling, and with a certain pride once said that he had made the great pay their court to him, and that with them he had always preserved his dignity." He thus verified what, as we saw alone, he had said to Goethe: "You must let them clearly understand what they possess in you."

The "assistance" he longed for came in the form of presents from monarchs, especially of the "magnanimous" one of the Empress of Russia, for whom he, at that time, wrote the polonaise, op. 89. These presents enabled him to make a permanent investment of twenty thousand marks, which his friends were very much surprised to find he owned, after his death. But, although by "decree" he drew yearly the sum of 2,700 marks, his principal source of income continued to be derived from his intellectual labor; for his dearly beloved brother Karl died and left him, as an inheritance, so to speak, his eight-year-old son, named after his father—the mother not being a fit person to take care of the child, and, besides, not enjoying the best of reputations. Beethoven's struggles for his "son," the unfortunate nephew, with the mother, whom he was wont to call the "queen of the night," filled the next succeeding years of his life with legal controversies and negotiations to such an extent that they seem to have hindered him in his work. Extreme trouble of mind, brought about by the social and political degeneration of Vienna immediately after the Congress, soon entirely obscured the lustre of the days we have just described; and it was only for short moments of time, as on the occasion of the celebrated concert of the year 1824, that we see his old pride and fame revive. The works performed at that concert were the *Missa Solemnis* and the Ninth Symphony. The former was a token of gratitude and devotion to the Archduke Rudolph, but at the same time a reflection of the soul of the artist himself as we have heard him describe it above. The symphony was written "for London," whither in these saddening times his eyes were directed, and which, although he never undertook the contemplated journey thither, became the incentive to the composition of many important works.

Among the works which date from 1814 and 1815, we may mention the sonata, op. 90, a "struggle between the head and the heart," addressed in the summer of 1814 to Count Moritz Lichnowsky on the occasion of his marriage to a Vienna singer; the song *Merkenstein* (op. 100), composed in the winter of 1814; Tiedge's *Hoffnung* (op. 94), composed after the last court concert for the singer Wild; the chorus *Meeresstille* and *Glueckliche Fahrt* (op. 112), which was written in 1815, and in 1822, "most respectfully dedicated to the immortal Goethe;" lastly, the magnificent cello sonatas, op. 102, dedicated to Countess Erdoedy, who became reconciled with him once more during this winter, after there had been a variance between them for a time. He calls the first of these sonatas the "free sonata," and, indeed, freedom now became the characteristic of his higher artistic pictures. The *adagio* of the second discloses to us, in the choral-like construction of its theme, the prevailing religious direction taken by his thoughts, which is also apparent in very many expressions and quotations to be found in his diary.

We have already mentioned the *Liederkreis*, op. 98. Beethoven worked at it and at the sonata op. 101 at the same time. The latter, an expression of the deepest poetry of the soul, was ready the following year, and was dedicated to Madame von Ertmann, his "dear Dorothea Caecilia," who, because she thoroughly understood the meaning of Beethoven's music, became a real propagandist of his compositions for the piano. In 1831, Mendelssohn could say that he had "learned much" from her deeply expressive execution. The noble lady had lost her only son during the absence of her husband in the wars of emancipation; and Beethoven had rescued her from a condition of mind bordering on melancholy, by coming to her and playing for her until she burst into tears. "The spell was broken." "We finite creatures with an infinite mind are born only for suffering and for joy; and we might almost say that the best of human kind obtain joy only through their sorrow." Thus spoke Beethoven to Countess Erdoedy, and this little incident confirms its truth. His own sufferings gave our artist the tones of his musical creations, and these creations were to him "the dearest gift of heaven," and, as it were, a consolation from on high.

But to continue our biography.

When, after a violent contest with the mother, he was made sole guardian of his nephew, and could then call him his own, he seems, as a lady whose diary is embodied in the little book *Eine stille Liebe zu Beethoven*, informs us, to gain new life. He devoted himself heart and soul to the boy, and he wrote, or was unable to write, according as the care of his nephew brought him joy or sorrow. We can readily understand how it came to pass that he now penned the words found by the lady just mentioned, in a memorandum book of his: "My heart overflows at the aspect of the beauties of nature—and this without her." His "distant loved one" was still to him the most valued possession of his life—more to him, even, than himself.

He had now in view several great projects—among them an opera, *Romulus*, by Treitschke, and an oratorio for the recently founded "Society of the Friends of Music," in Vienna. The latter failed, through the niggardliness of the directors, and the former was not finished, although our artist never gave up the intention of completing it. In the autumn of 1816, an English general, Kyd, asked Beethoven to write a symphony, for two hundred ducats. But as the general wanted it written in the style of his earlier works, Beethoven himself refused to accept the commission. Yet this narrow English enthusiast had excited Beethoven's imagination with glowing accounts of the harvest of profit he might reap in England, and as Beethoven had recently sold many of his works there, and as, besides, the new "Philharmonic Society" had handsomely remunerated him for these overtures, his intention of crossing the Channel began to assume a more definite form. His *Schlachtsymphonie* ("Battle-symphony"), especially, had already met with a very flattering reception in England. And a project was on foot in that country, even now, to give him a "benefit" by the production of his own works; and such a "benefit" was actually given for him there when he was on his death-bed. He wrote in 1816 that it would flatter him to be able to write some new works, such as symphonies and an oratorio, for the Society which embraced a greater number of able musicians than almost any other in Europe.

His diary covering this period to 1818, published in the work *Die Beethovenfeier und die Deutsche Kunst*, because of the many items of interest it has in it, contains these characteristic lines: "Drop operas and everything else. Write only in your own style." But even the sketches of the Seventh Symphony had the remark

Beethoven in 1824, age 54, two years before his death. (Image/caption by the editor.)

accompanying them: "2. Symphony in D minor," and those of the eighth: "Symphony in D minor—3. Symphony." Belonging to the years succeeding 1812, we find drafts of the *scherzo* of the Ninth Symphony. The headings above given undoubtedly had reference to this last, but the sketches of the first movement, decisive of the character of such a work, are not to be found until the year 1816, but then they are found with the physiognomy so masculine and so full of character which distinguishes this "symphony for London." He once said of Englishmen that they were, for the most part, "clever fellows;" and he—of whom Zelter wrote to Goethe, that "he must have had a man for his mother"—felt that, in England, he, as a man, had to do with men, and, as an artist, to enter the list with Handel, whose own powerful influence was due to his decided manfulness of character. And then, had not England produced a tragic poet like Shakespeare, whom Beethoven loved above all others? Deep, tragic earnestness, and a masculine struggle with fate, are here the fundamental tone and design of the whole. "And then a cowl when thou closest thy unhappy life"—such is the conclusion of the lines quoted above, in which he says that he must write "only in his own style."

And now, in July, 1817, came from London the "direct commission" he had so long endeavored to obtain. The Society desired to send him a proof of their esteem and gratitude for the many happy moments his works had given them to enjoy, and invited him to come to London to write two great symphonies, promising him an honorarium of three hundred pounds sterling. Beethoven immediately accepted the commission, and assured them that he would do his very best to execute it—honorable as it was to him, and coming as it did from so select a Society of artists—in the worthiest manner possible. He promised to go to work immediately. "He believed that he could nowhere receive the distinction which his gigantic genius—in advance of his age by several centuries—deserved, as he could in Great Britain. The respect shown him by the English people, he valued more than that of all Europe besides. The feeling he had of his own powers may, indeed, have contributed to make him prefer the English nation to all others, especially as they showered so many marks of distinction on him." Thus writes one of his most intimate friends in Vienna, Baron Von Zmeskall, already mentioned; and certain it is that he did his very best on this work. It, as well as the symphony in C minor, is of the true Beethoven type—more so, perhaps, than any other of his works—the full picture of his own personal existence and of the tragedy of human life in general. This work was followed by the Tenth Symphony, the "poetical idea," at least, of which we know. The first movement was intended to represent a "feast of Bacchus," the *adagio* a *cantique ecclesiastique*, a church hymn, and the *finale* the reconciliation of the antique world, which he esteemed so highly with the spirit of Christianity, into the full depth of which he came to have a deeper insight every day that passed. We see that he had lofty plans, and that no poet ever soared to sublimer heights than he. We must bear these great plans and labors of Beethoven in mind if we would rightly understand his subsequent life—if we would comprehend how, in the desolate and distracted existence he was compelled henceforth to lead, he did not become a victim of torpidity, but that, on the contrary, the elasticity of his genius grew greater and greater, and that his creations gained both in depth and perfection.

Thus do we see with our own eyes at least one of his works born of his own life.

The songs *Ruf vom Berge* and *So oder so*, were composed in the winter of 1816-17; and in the following spring, after the sudden death of one of his friends, the chorus *Rasch tritt der Tod*, from Schiller's Tell. "O God, help me! Thou seest me forsaken by all mankind. O hard fate, O cruel destiny! No, no, no, my unhappy condition will never end. Thou hast no means of salvation but to leave here. Only by so doing canst thou rise to the height of thy art. Here thou art immersed in vulgarity. Only one symphony, and then away, away, away!" Thus does he write in his diary. He next, in

1817, finished the quintet fugue, op. 137, and, in 1818, the great sonata for the Hammer-clavier, op. 106. The *adagio* of the latter is the musical expression of earnest prayer to God. Its first movement shows how he had soared once more to the heights of his art. "The sonata was written under vexatious circumstances," he says to his friend Ries; and to a younger fellow-artist, the composer Schnyder von Wartensee: "Go on. There is no calmer, more unalloyed or purer joy than that which arises from ascending higher and higher into the heaven of art." Such, too, was his mood in those days when he promised his friend Zmeskall the trio for the piano in C minor, his op. 1, worked over into the quintet op. 104; for he wrote: "I rehearse getting nearer the grave, without music, every day." In keeping with this is the song, *Lisch ans mein Licht*, "Put out my light," which also belongs to this period. The supplication: "O hear me always, Thou unspeakable One, hear me, thy unhappy creature, the most unfortunate of all mortals," found in his diary, belongs to this same time. It is now easy to see that he was in a very suitable frame of mind when he resolved, in 1818, to write a solemn mass for the occasion of the inauguration of his distinguished pupil as Archbishop of Olmutz. It was the "little court," the "little orchestra" for which he wished to write the music "for the honor of the Almighty, the Eternal, the Infinite;" for the Archduke thought of making him his *capellmeister* there. After four years' labor, the *Missa Solemnis*, op. 123, was finished. Beethoven called it " *l'oeuvre le plus accompli*, my most finished work." And, like the *Fidelio*, it is deserving of this characterization, but more on account of the pains taken with it and the labor expended on it than of its matter.

"Sacrifice again all the trivialities of social life to thy art. O, God above all! For Providence eternal omnisciently orders the happiness or unhappiness of mortal men." With these words from the Odyssey, he resolved to consecrate himself to this great work. And it was a resolve in very deed. For, as in opera, he knew that he was here bound by traditional forms—forms which, indeed, in some details afforded rich food to his own thoughts, but which, on the

An actual leaf from one of Beethoven's composition sketch books. The nearly indecipherable musical notation is a section from *Egmont*, written in 1809. (Image/caption by the editor.)

whole, hindered the natural flow of his fancy. We now approach a period in Beethoven's life in which he was strangely secluded from the world. The painter, Kloeber, the author of the best known portrait of Beethoven, and which is to be found in *Beethoven's Brevier*—it was painted during the summer of 1818—once saw him throw himself under a fir tree and look for a long time "up into the heavens." In some of the pages of his written conversations—for it was now necessary for him to have recourse to putting his conversations on paper more frequently on account of his increasing deafness—he wrote in the winter of 1819-20: "Socrates and Jesus were patterns to me;" and after that: "The moral law within us and the starry heavens above us.—Kant!!!" Just as on the 4th of March, 1820, he wrote:

"Ernte bald an Gottes Thron
Meiner Leiden schoenen Lohn."

This was the time of the struggles with the mother of his "son" and of the heartfelt sorrow he had to endure on account of the moral ruin of the poor boy himself, who, always going from the one to the other, did not really know to whom he belonged, and who, therefore, deceived both. "From the heart—may it in turn appeal to hearts!" He wrote these words on the score of the mass; and Schindler, who was now his companion, says that "the moment he began this work his whole nature seemed to change." He would sit in the eating-house sunk in deep thought, forget to order his meals, and then want to pay for them. "Some say he is a fool," wrote Zelter to Goethe in 1819. And Schindler tells us "he actually seemed possessed in those days, especially when he wrote the fugue and the *Benedictus*." That fugue, *Et vitam senturi* ("life everlasting!") is the climax of the work, since the depiction of the imperishableness and inexhaustibleness of Being was what Beethoven's powerful mind was most used to. The wonderful *Benedictus*, (Blessed is he who cometh in the name of the Lord) whose tones seem to float down from heaven to earth, the bestowal of help from on high, was subsequently the model used by Wagner for his descent of the Holy Grail, the symbol of divine grace, in the prelude to the *Lohengrin*. "When I recall his state of mental excitement, I must confess that I never before, and never after this period of his complete forgetfulness of earth, observed anything like it in him." So says Schindler. They had gone to visit him in Baden, near by, whither he repaired in the interest of his health, and where he loved so well to "wander through the quiet forest of firs" and think out his works. It was four o'clock in the afternoon. The door was closed, and they could hear him "singing, howling, stamping" at the fugue. After they had listened to this "almost horrible" scene, the door opened, and Beethoven stood before them, with trouble depicted on his countenance. He looked as if he had just gone through a struggle of life and death. "Pretty doings here; everybody is gone, and I have not eaten a morsel since yesterday noon," he said. He had worked the previous evening until after midnight; and so the food had grown cold and the servants left in disgust.

His work assumed greater and greater dimensions as he himself gradually rose to the full height of the subject. He no longer thought of completing it for the installation ceremonies. It became a grand fresco painting—a symphony in choruses on the words of the mass. He now began to work more calmly, and to compose at intervals other works, in order to quiet his over-excited mind and to earn a living for his "dear " nephew. And thus, while he was composing his mass, he produced not only the *Variirten Themen*, op. 105 and 107, which Thompson, of Edinburg—who had sent Beethoven the Scotch songs like op. 108 to be arranged—had ordered, but also the three *Last Sonatas*, op. 109, dedicated to Bettina's niece, Maximiliane Brentano, to whose excellent father he was indebted for ready assistance during these years of his pecuniary embarrassment; also op. 110, which was finished at Christmas, 1821, as op. 111 was on the 13th of January, 1822. It is said that he entertained a higher opinion himself of these sonatas than of his previous ones. They are greatly superior, however, only in some of their movements; and they are written in the grand, free style of that period, especially the *arietia* in the last opus, the variations of which are real pictures of his own soul. In the intervals between them, however, we find some trifles such as the *Bagatellen*, op. 119, which his pecuniary condition made it imperative he should compose, since, "as a brave knight by his sword, he had to live by his pen." And even the "33 *Veraenderungen*" ("Variations"), op. 120, on the works of Diabelli, of the year 1822-23, are more the intellectual play of the inexhaustible fancy of an artist than the work of the genuine gigantic creative power which Beethoven undoubtedly possessed. He had overtaxed his strength working on the mass, and thus exhausted it for a moment. The two chorus-songs, op. 121b and op. 122, the *Opferlied* and *Bundeslied*, which date from the year 1822-23, bear the stamp of occasional compositions, which they, in fact, are.

But in the meantime the lion had roused himself again. He now only needed to give the finishing touch to the Mass, and in the spring of 1823 the entire work was completed. The summer of 1822 found him fully engaged on the composition of that monument to his genius, the Ninth Symphony. Freedom from the torment of exhausting labor, and the entire surrender of himself to "his own style," gave his fancy back its old elasticity and all its productive power. Scarcely any year of his life was more prolific of works than this year 1822. "Our Beethoven seems again to take a greater interest in music, which, since the trouble with his hearing began to increase, he avoided almost as a woman-hater avoids the sex. To the great pleasure of all, he improvised a few tunes in a most masterly manner." Thus do we read in the Leipsig *Musikzeitung*, in the spring of 1822, and the Englishman, John Russell, gives us a charming description of such an evening in the Cotta *Beethovenbuch*. Weisse's droll poem, *Der Kuss* ("The Kiss") op. 128, is found among the serious sketches of this year. And now he received a whole series of commissions. An English captain, named Reigersfeld, wanted a quartet, and Breitkopf and Haertel an operatic poem worthy of his art, before he "hung up his harp forever." Others asked for other kinds of music. "In short," he writes to his brother Johann, "people are fighting to get works from me, happy, unhappy man

Portrait of Beethoven with his signature. (Image/caption by the editor.)

that I am. If my health is good, I shall yet be able to feather my nest." Friederich Rochlitz brought him, too, a commission from Breitkopf and Haertel to write "music for Faust." Rochlitz gives us a very interesting account of Beethoven's appearance and whole mode of life at this time. Not Beethoven's neglected, almost savage exterior, he says, not his bushy black hair, which hung bristling about his head, would have stirred him; what stirred him was the whole appearance of the deaf man who, notwithstanding his infirmity, brought joy to the hearts of millions—pure, intellectual joy. But when he received the commission, he raised his hand high up and exclaimed: "That might be worth while. But I have been intending for some time to write three other great works—two great symphonies, very different from each other, and an oratorio. I shudder at the thought of beginning works of such magnitude. But once engaged on them, I shall find no difficulty." He spoke of the Ninth Symphony, to which he had now begun to give the finishing touches, in all earnestness.

This was interrupted for a short time by the overture, *Zur Weihe des Hauses* (op. 124), for the opening of the renovated Josephstadt theater with the "Ruins of Athens," of 1812. It is the portal to the temple in which art is praised as something consecrated to the service of mankind—as a thing which may lift us for blissful moments into the region of the purifying and elevating influences of higher powers. Even in this work, which dates from September, 1822, we may hear the solemn sound and rhythm of the Ninth Symphony. And, indeed, after a memorandum on the "Hungarian Story," we find in the sketches of it the words, "Finale, *Freude schoener Goetterfunken,*" together with the wonderfully simple melody itself, which sounds to humanity's better self like the music of its own redemption. Beethoven's own nature was deeply moved at this time. Weber's *Freischuetz,* with Wilhelmine Schroeder, afterwards so celebrated, had excited the greatest enthusiasm. Rossini's reception in Vienna was "like an opeotheosis;" and Beethoven was determined to let the light of his genius shine forth, which he could do only by writing a work "in his own style." The world was "his for another evening," and he was anxious to turn that evening to account. And, indeed, had he not a world of sorrows to paint—sorrows which actual life had brought to him? He had also a world of joys—joys vouchsafed to him by his surrendering of himself to a higher life.

An incident which occurred during this fall of 1822 tells us something of this gloomy night of his personal existence. Young Schroeder-Devrient, encouraged by her success with *Pamina* and *Agathe*, had chosen the *Fidelio* for her benefit, and Beethoven himself was to wield the baton. Schindler tells us how, even during the first scene of the opera, everything was in confusion, but that no one cared to utter the saddening words: "It's impossible for you, unfortunate man." Schindler finally, in response to Beethoven's own questioning, wrote something to that effect down. In a trice, Beethoven leaped into the parterre, saying only: "Quick, out of here!" He ran without stopping to his dwelling, threw himself on the sofa, covered his face with his two hands, and remained in that position until called to table. But, even at table, he did not utter a word. He sat at it, the picture of the deepest melancholy. Schindler's account of the incident closes thus: "In all my experience with Beethoven, this November day is without a parallel. It mattered not what disappointments or crosses misfortune brought him, he was ill-humored only for moments, sometimes depressed. He would, however, soon be himself again, lift his head proudly, walk about with a firm step, and rule in the workshop of his genius. But he never fully recovered from the effect of this blow."

The performance itself brought out, for the first time, in all its completeness, musicodramatic art, in the representation of the scene, "Kill first his wife." Richard Wagner, who has so highly developed this musicodramatic art, admits that he acquired the real idea of plastic shaping for the stage from Schroeder-Devrient. To it, also, Beethoven owed it that he was invited, during the same winter (1822-23), to compose a new opera. It was Grillparzer's *Melusine*, but the intention to compose it was never carried into effect.

We have now reached the zenith of the life of Beethoven as an artist. Besides the Ninth Symphony, he finished only the five last quartets which beam in their numerous movements like "the choir

The New Year greeting card that Beethoven gave to Baroness Dorothea Ertmann in 1804. (Image/caption by the editor.)

of stars about the sun." The welcome incentive to the composition of these last came to him just at this time from the Russian, Prince Gallitzin, who gave him a commission to write them, telling him at the same time to ask what remuneration he wished for his work. But the Symphony filled up the next following year, 1823. Nothing else, except the "fragmentary ideas" of the *Bagatellen*, op. 126, engaged him during that time.

"To give artistic form only to what we wish and feel, that most essential want of the nobler of mankind," it is, as he wrote himself to the Archduke at this time, that distinguishes this mighty symphony, and constitutes, so to speak, the sum and substance of his own life and intuition. This symphony was soon connected in popular imagination with Goethe's Faust, as representing the tragic course of human existence.

And when we bear in mind how closely related just here the musician was to the poet, this interpretation of the work, given first by Richard Wagner on the occasion of its presentation in 1846 in Dresden, seems entirely warranted. What was there of which life had not deprived him? The words it had always addressed to him were these words from Faust: *Entbehren sollst du, sollst entbehren* ("Renounce thou must, thou must renounce"). He now wished to paint a full picture of this vain struggle with relentless fate in tones, and what he had just gone through in his own experience enabled him to do it in living colors. All the recollections of his youth crowded upon him. There were the "pretty lively blonde" whom he had met in Bonn; Countess Giulietta, who had a short time before returned to Bonn with her husband; and his "distant loved one" in Berlin! A promenade through the lovely Heiligenstadt valley, in the spring of 1823, brought to his mind anew pictures of the reconciling power of nature, as well as of the *Pastorale* and the C minor symphony. He was now able to form an idea of their common meaning, and to put an interpretation on them very different from his first idea and first interpretation of them. He began to have a much deeper insight into the ultimate questions and enigmas of existence.

But, all of a sudden, his humor left him. He refused to receive any visitors. "Samothracians, come not here; bring no one to me," he wrote to Schindler, from the scene of his quiet life in the country. What had never happened before, even when he was in the highest stages of intellectual exaltation, now came to pass: he repeatedly returned from his wanderings through the woods and fields without his hat. "There is nothing higher than to approach nearer to the Deity than other men, and from such proximity to spread the rays of the Deity among the human race." In these words, directed to the Archduke Rudolph, he summed up his views of his art and what he wished to accomplish in it. It was everything to him—a language, consolation, admonition, light and prophecy.

This we learn most clearly from the Ninth Symphony, which he finished at this time, in Baden.

From the dark abyss of nothing arises the Will, infinite Will; and with it the struggles and the sorrow of life. But it is no longer personal sorrow—for what is personal sorrow compared with the sorrow of the world as known to a great mind, experienced by a great heart?—it is the struggle for a higher existence which we "mortals have to engage in against the infinite spirit." "Many a time did I curse my Creator because he has made his creatures the victims of the merest accidents." Cries of anguish and anger like this—the cries of great souls whose broad vision is narrowed by the world, and whose powerful will is hampered—find utterance here. "I shall take fate by the jaws," he says again, and how immense is the struggle as well as the consciousness of a higher, inalienable possession, which lives as a promise in the breasts of all! Such blows, murmurs, prayers, longings, such despair; and then, again, such strength and courage after trial, had never before been expressed in music. In the Ninth Symphony, we hear the voices of the powers which through all ages have been the makers of history; of the powers which preserve and renovate the life of humanity; and so the Will, the Intellect, man, after a terrible effort and concentration of self, stands firmly before us, bold and clear-eyed—for Will is the world itself.

But when we see the man Beethoven, we find him divided against himself. We have often heard him say that he found the world detestable; and we shall again hear him express his opinion on that subject plainly enough, in this his work.

In the second movement, which he himself calls only *allegro vivace*, and which, indeed, is no *scherzo*, not even a Beethoven-like one, but rather a painting, we have a dramatic picture of the earthly world in the whirl of its pleasures, from the most ingenuous joy of mere existence—such as he himself frequently experienced in such fullness that he leaped over chairs and tables—to the raging, uncontrollable Bacchanalian intoxication of enjoyment. But we have in it also a fresco-painting of the "dear calmness of life," of joy in the existing, of exultation and jubilation as well as of the demoniacal in sensuous life and pleasure. But what nutriment and satisfaction this splendid symphony affords to a noble mind! It carries such a man from the arms of pleasure to "the stars," from art to nature, from appearance to reality.

This ideal kingdom of the quiet, sublime order of the world,

The only known painting of Beethoven from life. The artist, Joseph Karl Stieler (1781-1858), created it between 1819 and 1820, when Beethoven was around 50 years old. (Image/caption by the editor.)

which calms our minds and senses, and expresses our infinite longings, is heard in the *adagio* of the work. And when, in an incomparably poetical union to the quiet course of the stars and to the eternally ordered course of things, the longing, perturbed human heart is contrasted by a second melody, with a wealth of inner beauty never before imagined, we at last see the soul, so to speak, disappear entirely before itself, dissolved in the sublimity of the All. The steps of time, expressed by the rhythm of the final chords, sound like the death knell of the human heart. Its wants and wishes are silenced in the presence of such sublimity, and sink to naught.

But the world is man, is the heart, and wants to live, to live! And so here the final echo is still the longing, sounding tones of human feeling.

Beethoven himself tells us the rest of the development of this powerful tragedy, and thus confirms the explanation of it we have given, as well as the persistence of ultimate truth in his own heart; for in it we find—after the almost raging cry of all earthly existence in the orchestral storm of the beginning of the *finale*, which was even then called a "feast of scorn at all that is styled human joy"—in the sketches, as text to the powerful recitatives of the contra-bassos: "No, this confusion reminds us of our despairing condition. This is a magnificent day. Let us celebrate it with song." And then follows the theme of the first movement: "O no, it is not this; it is something else that I am craving. The will and consciousness of man are at variance the one with the other, and the cause of man's despairing situation." Next comes the *motive* for the *scherzo*: "Nor is it this thing either; it is but merriness and small talk"—the trifles of sensuous pleasure. Next comes the theme of the *adagio*: "Nor is it this thing either," and thereupon the words: "I myself shall sing—music must console us, music must cheer us;" and then the melody, *Freude schoener Goetterfunken*, is heard, expressive of the newly won peace of the soul, descriptive of human character in the full beauty of its simplicity and innocence restored. Beethoven knew from what depths of human nature music was born, and what its ultimate meaning to mankind is.

We are made to experience this more fully still by the continuation of the *finale* which represents the solution of the conflict of this tragedy of life. For the "joy" that is here sung plainly springs from its only pure and lasting source, from the feeling of all-embracing love—that feeling which, as religion, fills the heart. The *Ihr stuertz nieder Millionen* is the foundation, the germ (to express it in the language of music of double counterpoint) of the *Seid umschlungen, Millionen*, and then the whole sings of joy as the transfiguration of the earthly world by eternal love. The will can accomplish nothing greater than to sacrifice itself for the good of the whole. To our great artist, the greatest and most wonderful phenomenon in the world was not the conqueror but the overcomer of the world; and he knew that this spirit of love cannot die.

The last grand piano owned by Beethoven. (Image/caption by the editor.)

This is celebrated by the *finale* as the last consequence of the "struggle with fate," of man's life-struggle. Is it claiming too much to say that out of the spirit of this music a "new civilization " and an existence more worthy of human beings might be developed, since it leads us back to the foundation and source of civilization and human existence—to religion? Beethoven was one of those great minds who have added to the intellectual possessions of our race in regions which extend far beyond the merely beautiful in art. When we bear this in mind, we can understand why he wanted to write a tenth symphony as the counterpart and final representation of these highest conceptions of the nature and goal of our race. This tenth symphony he intended should transfigure the merely humanly beautiful of the antique world in the light of the refined humanity of modern ideas—the earthly in the light of the heavenly. And we may understand, too, what we are told of himself, that as soon as cheerfulness beamed in his countenance, it shed about him all the charms of childlike innocence. "When he smiled," we are told, "people believed not only in him, but in humanity." Occasionally there would blossom on his lips a smile which those who saw could find no other word to describe but "heavenly." So full was his heart of hearts of the highest treasure of humanity.

We shall see how the last quartets, which follow now, represent this, his sublime transfigured condition of soul, in the most varied pictures, and disclose it to the very bottom.

Of works composed during this period, we may mention: March to "Tarpeja " and the *Bardengeist* composed in 1813; *Gute NachTicht*, *Elegischer Gesang*, *Kriegers Abschied*, composed in 1814; Duos for the clarionette and bassoon, which appeared in 1815; *Es ist vollbracht*, *Sehnsucht*, Scotch songs, composed in 1815; *Der Mann von Wort*, op. 99. *Militaermarsch*, composed in 1816; quintet op. 104 (after op. 1, III), composed in 1817; *Clavierstueck* in B, composed in

Sketches of Beethoven by German illustrator Ludwig Peter August Burmeister (1804-1870)—best known by the pseudonym, Johann Peter Lyser. (Image/caption by the editor.)

1818; *Gratulationsmenuet*, composed in 1822. It will be noticed that the number of his works grows steadily smaller according as their volume or their depth of meaning grows greater. This last will be evident especially from his subsequent quartets which, so to speak, stand entirely alone.

CHAPTER V

NOBLE SOULS FALL usually only because they do not know the mournful but incontestable truth that, considering our present customs and political institutions, the artist has more to suffer in proportion as he is a genuine artist. The more original and gigantic his works are, the more severely is he punished for the effects they produce. The swifter and sublimer his thoughts, the more does he vanish from the dim vision of the multitude." Thus did Beethoven's direct successor in art, Hector Berlioz, complain at the end of his days; and to whom can what he says here be applied with more propriety than to our artist, especially at this period of his life, when his thoughts took their sublimest flight? His action now seemed indeed to assure him unconditional victory, even in his immediate environment—we are approaching the celebrated concert of May, 1824—but how soon shall we see him again misunderstood by the crowd and, as a consequence, lonelier than ever before.

Another Beethoven portrait with signature. (Image/caption by the editor.)

He had again enjoyed to the full the "higher life which art and science imply, and which they give it to us to hope for;" and he, in consequence, became exceedingly neglectful of himself; so that his brother found it necessary to say to him: "You must buy yourself a new hat tomorrow. The people make merry at your expense because you have so bad a hat." But now that the "colossal creation" was finished, even to the last iota, he began to be in better humor, to stroll about the streets gazing at the show-windows, and to salute many an old friend, as, for instance, his former teacher, Schenk, more warmly. His name was now more frequently on the lips of friends, and when it was known that a great symphony, as well as the Mass, was finished, people recalled the boundless rapture of the years 1813-14; and a letter signed by men of the higher classes of society—men whom Beethoven himself loved and honored—invited him, in February, 1824, to abstain no longer from the performance of something great. And, indeed, the Italian *roulade* and all kinds of purely external *bravoura* had obtained supremacy in Vienna. The "second childhood of taste" threatened to follow the "golden age of art." It was hoped that home art would receive new life from Beethoven, who, in his own sphere, had no equal, and that, thanks to his influence, the true and the beautiful would rule supreme again.

Schindler found him with the manuscript in his hand. "It is very pretty! I am glad!" Beethoven said, in a very peculiar tone. And another hope was bound up with this. He hoped to obtain compensation for his long labor, and, in this way, leisure to produce something new worthy of his genius. The preparation for the concert was attended by very much that was disagreeable. His own want of resolution and suspicious manner contributed their share to this. With the most splenetic humor, he writes: "After six weeks' vexation, I am boiled, stewed, roasted." And when several of his more intimate friends, like Count Lichnowsky, Schuppanzigh and Schindler, resorted to a little subterfuge to make him come to some resolve, he said: "I despise deceit. Visit me no more. And let him visit me no more. I'm not giving a party." But, on the other hand, the first violinists of the city—Schuppanzigh, Mayseder and Boehm, who is still living—together with *capellmeister* Umlauf, were at the head of the orchestra, while a large number of amateurs were ready to lend their assistance at a moment's notice. Their motto was: "Anything and everything for Beethoven!" And thus the preparations for the performance of Beethoven's great creations were begun.

"Just as if there were words beneath them?" asked Schindler, speaking of the powerful recitatives of the basses in the Ninth Symphony. Henriette Sontag and Caroline Unger, both subsequently so celebrated, found it exceedingly difficult to execute the solos in the Mass and the *finale*; but to all prayers that they might be changed, Beethoven had only one answer: "No!" To which Henriette finally replied: "Well, in God's name, let us torment ourselves a little longer, take a little more trouble, and attempt it." The performance was to occur on the 7th of May. That "rare, noble man," Brunswick had, as he said, brought "four ears" with him, that he might not lose a single note. Frau von Ertmann was again in Vienna. The boxes were all soon taken, and many seats were sold at a premium. Beethoven personally invited the court. His trusted servant, who was specially helpful to him on this occasion, said to him: "We shall take your green coat with us, too; the theater is dark; no one can see us. O my great master, not a black dress coat have you in your possession." The house was crowded to overfullness. Only the court box was almost empty, on account of the Emperor's absence. Beethoven's attendant again tells us: "His reception was more than imperial; at the fourth round of applause, the people became vociferous." And Boehm tells us how the tears rushed into his own and Mayseder's eyes at the very beginning. And what a success the performance was!

In one of the accounts of it that have come down to us, we read: "Never in my life did I hear such tempestuous and at the same time such hearty applause. At one place—where the kettle-drums so boldly take up the rhythmic motive alone—the second movement of the symphony was totally interrupted by the applause; the tears stood in the eyes of the performers; Beethoven, however, contrived to wield the baton until Umlauf called his attention to the action of the audience by a motion of his hand. He looked at them and bowed in a very composed way." At the close the applause was greater still. Yet, strange to say, the man who was the cause of it all again turned his back to the enthusiastic audience. At this juncture, the happy thought occurred to Unger to wheel Beethoven about towards the audience, and to ask him to notice their applause with their waving of hats and handkerchiefs. He testified his gratitude simply by bowing, and this was the signal for the breaking forth of a jubilation such as had scarcely ever before been heard in a theater, and which it seemed would never end. The next day, we read, in his conversation leaves, what some one said to him: "Everybody is shattered and crushed by the magnitude of your works."

And now, what of the pecuniary success of the performance? It was measured by about one hundred and twenty marks. The expenses attending it had been too great. Besides, regular subscribers, entitled to their seats in boxes, did not pay a farthing for this concert. The court did not send in a penny, which, however, they were wont not to fail to do on the occasion of the commonest benefits. When Beethoven reached his home, Schindler handed him the account of the receipts. "When he saw it, he broke down entirely. We took him and laid him on the sofa. We remained at his side until late in the night. He asked neither for food nor for anything else. Not an audible word did he utter. At last, when we observed that Morpheus had gently closed his eyes, we retired. His servant found him next morning in his concert toilette (his green dress coat) in the same place, asleep." This account is by Schindler, who, together with the young official, Joseph Huettenbrenner, one of Franz Schubert's intimate friends, had taken him home on this occasion.

This was the first performance of the *Missa Solemnis* (op. 123) and of the Ninth Symphony (op. 125). It took place on the 7th of May, 1824. The fact that when the performance was repeated on the 24th of May, spite of the additional attraction of the "adored" tenor, David, who sang Rossini's *Di tanti palpiti*, (after so much pain), the house was half empty, shows that, after all, it was more curiosity to see the celebrated deaf man than real taste for art which had filled it the first time. Like Mozart, Beethoven did not live long enough to

The room in which Beethoven was born on or around December 17, 1770, in Bonn, Germany. (Image/caption by the editor.)

pluck even the pecuniary fruits of his genius. Not till 1845 did the magnanimous liberality of one who was really permeated by his spirit bring it to pass that a monument was erected to him in his native city, Bonn, as that same liberality has brought it to pass that one has been erected to him, in our own day, in his second home, Vienna. We have reference to the royal gift and to the equally rich playing of Franz Liszt.

It now became more imperative for him to give his attention to those compositions which promised him some immediate return, to the quartets, to write which he had received a commission from persons as noted for their generosity to him as for their love of art. These and the op. 127 occupy the first place in this brilliant constellation of art. "I am not writing what I should prefer to write. I am writing for the money I need. When that end is satisfied, I hope to write what is of most importance to myself and to art—Faust." He thus expressed himself when engaged in the composition of the Ninth Symphony, and there was some talk of his writing an "Oratorio for Boston." And so, likewise, the German Melusine and an opera for Naples, the Requiem, the tenth symphony, and an overture on B-A-C-H remained projects and no more. But they were also a great prospect for the future while he was engaged in the labors of the day; and they exercised no inconsiderable influence on the composition of the quartets themselves. The more he became interested in these works—and what works were better calculated to interest a composer of such poetic power—the more did these ideas become interwoven into the works themselves. They generated the peculiarly grand style and the monumental character which distinguish these last quartets. The soul-pictures from Faust especially are here eloquently re-echoed in the most sublime monologues. And, indeed, the Prince, who had given him the commission to write them, seemed to be the very man to induce Beethoven to achieve what was highest and best in art, even in such a narrow sphere. For he had so arranged it that, even before its production in Vienna, that "sublime masterpiece," the Mass, was publicly performed. He informs us that the effect on the public was indescribable; that he had never before heard anything, not even of Mozart's music, which had so stirred his soul; that Beethoven's genius was centuries in advance of his age, and that probably there was not among his hearers a single one enlightened enough to take in the full beauty of his music. On the other hand, there reigned in Vienna that weak revelry of the period of the restoration, with its idol Rossini, a revelry which had driven all noble and serious music into the background. Besides, the Prince had ordered that the costs for musical composition should be curtailed "to any desired sum."

Beethoven now went to work in earnest, and this composition was destined to be his last.

He had already made a great many drafts of the works above mentioned, one for op. 127 in the summer of 1822, one for the succeeding quartet in A minor (op. 131), in the year 1823, when he was completing the Ninth Symphony. Both op. 127 and the quartet in A minor remind us, in more ways than one, of the style of the Ninth Symphony—the latter by its passion so full of pain, the former, with its *adagio*, where the longing glances to the stars have generated a wonderful, melancholy peace of soul. The immediately following third quartet (op. 130) stands out before us like a newly created world, but one which is "not of this world." And, indeed, the events in Beethoven's life became calculated more and more to liberate him, heart and soul, from this world, and the whole composition of the quartets appears like a preparation for the moment when the mind, released from existence here, feels united with a higher being. But it is not a painfully happy longing for death that here finds expression. It is the heartfelt, certain and joyful feeling of something really eternal and holy that speaks to us in the language of a new dispensation. And even the pictures of the world here to be found, be they serious or gay, have this transfigured light—this outlook into eternity. There is little in the world of art, in which the nature of the religious appears so fully in its substance and essence without showing itself at any time otherwise than purely human, and therefore imperishable—never clothed in an accidental and perishable garb. This explains how a people not noted for any musical genius, but who are able to understand the spirit and meaning of music, the English, whom Beethoven himself esteemed so highly, considered his music "so religious." And, indeed, his music is religious in its ultimate meaning and spirit. This character of his music finds its purest and most striking expression in the last quartets; and these quartets enable us to understand the saying of Richard Wagner, Beethoven's truest pupil and successor, that our civilization might receive a new soul from the spirit of this music, and a renovation of religion which might permeate it through and through.

We now pass to an account of the details of the origin of these works.

The bitterness which Beethoven was destined henceforth to taste proceeded for the most part from his own relatives. "God is my witness, my only dream is to get away entirely from you, from my miserable brother, and from this despicable family which has been tied to me," he writes, in 1825, to his growing nephew. We cannot refrain from touching on these sad things, because now, especially, they exercised the greatest influence on his mind and on his pecuniary circumstances, and because they finally led to a catastrophe which played a part in bringing about his premature death.

His weak and "somewhat money-loving" brother, Johann, had, indeed, in consequence of Beethoven's own violent moral interference, married a silly wife. He found it impossible to control her course, or even to get a divorce from her, because he had made over to her a part of his property, and was "inflexible" on this very point. And so the brother was not able, spite of many invitations, to induce Beethoven to visit him even once on his estate of Wasserhof, near Gneixendorf, on the Danube. Ludwig wrote him, in the summer of 1823: "O accursed shame! Have you not a spark of manhood in you? Shall I debase myself by entering such company?" Yet, his sister-in-law was "tamed" by degrees. But the mother of the boy continued, now that he was beginning to mature, to draw him into her own baneful circle, and, as Beethoven wrote in the summer of 1824, into the poisonous breath of the dragon; and levity, falsehood and unbecoming behavior towards his uncle, who was at the same time a father to him, followed. Carried away by the impulses of his moral feelings, the latter was severe even to harshness with the boy, and yet could not dispense with the young man's company because of his increasing age and isolation.

The natural craving for love, moral severity and the consciousness of paternal duty, wove the texture of which our artist's shroud was made.

The correspondence of this year, 1824, turns principally upon the pecuniary realization from his new, great works; for he wanted to be in London in the fall without fail. We have also a letter of his about his will, to his lawyer, Dr. Bach, dated in the summer. He writes: "Only in divine art is the power which gives me the strength to sacrifice to the heavenly muses the best part of my life." We hear also the celestial sounds of the *adagio*, op. 127, ringing in our ears. He was himself filled with this true "manna;" for he exclaims in these same summer days, "Apollo and the muses will not yet allow me to be delivered over to the hands of death, for I yet owe them what the Spirit inspires me with and commands me to finish. I feel as if I had written scarcely a note." And we even now find the sketches of those pieces expressive of a happiness more than earthly, or else, in gay irony, of contempt for the existing world, or of the mighty building up of a new world; the *alla damza tedesca* and the *poco scherzando* of op. 130, as well as the great fugue, op. 133, which was intended to be the original *finale* of op. 130, and which, by its superscription, "overture" and the gigantic strides in its theme, reminds us of the plan of the

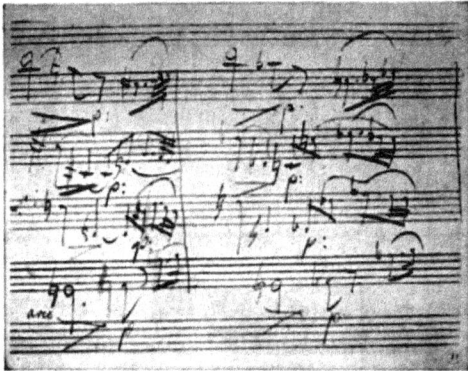

A page from one of Beethoven's composition sketch books, this one featuring his String Quartet No. 13 in B-flat Major, Opus 130, written in 1825. (Image/caption by the editor.)

Bachouverture. Even the unspeakably deep melancholy and, at the same time, blissful, hopeful *cavatine* of the same third quartet op.

130, blossoms forth now from the feeling of his heart, which has taken into itself the full meaning of the eternal, and is filled with a higher joy. We here find, as in the last tones of Mozart's soul, the germs of a new and deep-felt language of the heart, a real personal language, acquired to humanity for the expression of its deepest secrets, and which, in our own day, has led to the most touching soul-pictures in art—to the transfiguration of Isolde, and to Bruennhild's dying song of redeeming love.

A mighty seriousness overpowers him. The desolate horrors that surround him endow him with the power to understand more clearly the higher tasks of the mind in which his art had a living part. We see plainly that his nature tends more and more towards the one thing necessary—"All love is sympathy," sympathy with the sorrows of the world, says the philosopher. And so while his vision takes an immense sweep over the field of existence, we see that an inexhaustible source of patient goodness and of the kindest and most heartfelt love, springs, up within him. "From childhood up it was my greatest happiness to be able to work for others," he once said; and again when the overture, op. 24, was reproduced: "I was very much praised on this account, etc. But what is that all to the great Master of Tones above—above—above! rightly the Most High, when here below it is used only for purposes of ridicule. Most high dwarfs!!!" We here listen to the sublime irony of his tones in op. 130, but also to the lustrous mildness of the *adagio* of op. 127, in which in the little movement in E major, the human soul itself, filled with the spirit of the Eternal, so to speak, opens its eyes and looks upward. "I am what is, I am all that is, that was and that will be. No mortal man has lifted my veil. He comes from Himself alone, and to this Only One all things owe their existence." Beethoven wrote out this Egyptian saying in this summer of 1824, framed it and placed it on his writing table before him. He well knew what the really creative and preserving deity in human life is. That deity lived in his own most heartfelt thought and feeling. It was to him a continual source of bliss. It inspired his pen. To it he was indebted for the poetic creations which sprung unbidden from his brain.

The quartet in A minor, op. 132, belongs to the spring and summer of 1825. His journey to London had been postponed. Schindler gives as the reason of this, the "bad behavior of his dearly beloved nephew, which had become somewhat notorious." How could his "son" be abandoned, thus unguarded, to "the poisonous breath of the dragon?" But as the invitation was renewed, the Tenth Symphony was again taken in hand, and from the sketches of it now made, we know all that is certain about it. It was intended to do no less than to add the "beautiful to the good," to wed the spirit of Christianity to the beauty of the antique, or rather to transfigure the mere worldly beauty of the antique in the light of the superterrestrial. We find, indeed, a picture of this kind, a direct, intentional, higher picture of the world in the *adagio, in modo lidico*, in the second quartet. It is called the "Song of Thanksgiving of a Convalescent to the Deity," and is a choral between the repetitions of which, ever richer and more heartfelt, the joyful pulsations of new life are expressed. Beethoven had been seriously sick during this spring. His affection for his nephew had assumed, in consequence of one continual irritation of his feelings, the nature of a passion which tormented the boy to death, but which, like every passion, brought no happiness to Beethoven himself. The first movement of this quartet in A minor is a psychological picture—a poem of the passions—the consuming character of which can be explained only by this very condition of the artist's own soul. And how Beethoven's creations always came from his own great soul, that soul so fully capable of every shade of feeling and excitement! The account left us by the young poet, Rellstab, written in the spring of 1825, gives us a perfect description of the state Beethoven was in at this time. He describes him "a man with a kindly look, but a look also of suffering." Beethoven's own letters confirm the correctness of this description. "In what part of me am I not wounded and torn?" he cries out to his nephew, whose frivolity had already begun to bear evil fruit. On another occasion he said: "O, trouble me no more. The man with the scythe will not respite me much longer."

Notwithstanding this, however, or perhaps because of this extreme excitement of his whole nature, the summer of 1825 was very rich in productions. "Almost in spite of himself," he had to write the quartet in C sharp minor (op. 131); after that in B major (op. 130). The last quartet also, that in F major, had its origin in that "inexhaustible fancy"—a fancy which always tended to the production of such works. Hence it is that the number of movements increases. The second has five; the third (B major), six; and the fourth (C sharp minor), seven—as if the old form of the suite, or the *divertimento* of the septet was to be repeated. But a moment's comparison immediately shows the presence of the old organic articulation of the form of the sonata. These movements are in fact only transitions to, and connecting links between, two colossal movements. They increase the usual number of movements, although frequently nothing more than short

The Beethoven monument in the capitol city of Austria, Vienna. (Image/caption by the editor.)

sentences, and at times only a few measures. But the introductory movement and the finale in the quartet in A minor loom up like the pillars of Hercules, and determine the impassioned character and the dramatic style of the whole. Beethoven himself called it a piece of art worthy of him. The same may be said of op. 130, when the great fugue, op. 133, is considered a part of it, which in our day it should always be conceded to be. And how immensely great is this spirit when, in the quartet in C sharp minor, it awakes from the most profound contemplation of self to the contemplation of the world and its pain.—"Through sorrow, joy!"

We must refer the reader to the third volume of *Beethoven's Leben*, published in Leipzig in 1877, for a detailed account of the desolation of our artist, produced by the narrow circle with which the restoration of Metternich and Gentz surrounded him, at a time when his own mind and feeling were expanding to greater dimensions than ever before. To the same source we must send him for a description of the full earnestness and greatness of this last period in the life of our artist. In that work was for the first time presented to the public, from original sources, and especially from the records of Beethoven's written conversations, extant in the Berlin library, the comfortless—but at the same time, and spite of continual torment, intellectually exalted—picture of his character. "Words are interdicted. It is a fortunate thing that tones are yet free," wrote Ch. Kuffner, the poet of the oratorio, *Saul and David*, to him at this time—a work in which he wished to give expression both to his own relation as a human being to his "David," and to the wonderworking nature of his art. The execution of this plan was prevented only by death. The general demoralization which had invaded Vienna with the Congress made its effects felt directly in his own circle, through the agency of his nephew, and thus paved the way for disaster to himself. "Our age has need of vigorous minds to scourge these paltry, malicious, miserable wretches," he cries out at this very time to his nephew, who had permitted himself to make merry, in a manner well calculated to irritate, at the expense of a genuine *faijak*—as Beethoven was wont now to call the good Viennese—the music-dealer Haslinger; and the matter had become public. But he adds to the above: "Much as my heart resists causing pain to a single human being." And, indeed, his heart knew nothing of such anger or vengeance. It was always a real sympathizer with the sorrows born of human weakness—a sorrow which with him swelled to the dimensions of the world-sorrow itself. To this feeling his op. 130 in B major is indebted for its series of pictures, in which we see the world created, as it were, anew with a bold hand, with the ironic, smiling, melancholy, humorous, cheerful coloring of the several pieces—pieces which, indeed, are no mere sonata movements, but full pictures of life and of the soul. The *cavatina* overtops it as a piece of his own heart, which, as he admitted himself to K. Holz, always drew from him "fresh tears."

"Imitate my virtues, not my faults," he implores his "son." Speaking of the rabble of domestics, he says: "I have had to suffer the whole week like a saint;" and, on another occasion, still more painfully: "May God be with thee and me. It will be all over soon with thy faithful father." His days, so strangely divided between the loftiest visions of the spirit and the meanest troubles of life, henceforth render him more and more indifferent to the latter. We find persons invade his circle whom otherwise he would never have permanently endured about him, and who frequently led him into minor sorts of dissipation even in public places. This reacted on the nephew, whose respect for the character of his "great uncle" could not long stand a course of action apparently like his own. But even now we see a picture in tones of which one of the *faijaks*, the government officer and dilettante, Holz, who copied it, writes to Beethoven himself: "When one can survey it thus calmly, new worlds come into being." We have reference to the quartet in C sharp minor, op. 131. "With a look beaming with light, dripping with sorrow and joy," young Dr. Rollett saw him at this time in beautiful Baden, and, indeed, this work, which he himself called the "greatest" of his quartets, discloses to us, in a manner different from the Ninth Symphony, the meaning of his own life, which he here himself, as Richard Wagner has said, displayed to us, a wild melody of pleasure and pain. But we now recognize more clearly that something "like a vulture is devouring his heart." We, indeed, are drawing near to the catastrophe which led to his premature end.

As early as in the fall of 1825 he had witnessed "stormy scenes." An uncontrollable love of gaming and a habit of loitering about the

A portrait of Beethoven as he was nearing the end of his life. (Image/caption by the editor.)

streets had led the young man into worse and worse courses, to falsehood and embezzlement. And when these were discovered, he secretly ran away from home. It was not long, however, before the loving weakness of his uncle called him back. The only effect of this was henceforth to condemn Beethoven himself to a slavish, too slavish life, one which would have been a torment even to an ordinary mortal, but which must have been doubly so to a passionate, great man who was deaf. The nephew found fault with his uncle, with his "reproaches" and "rows." He accused him even of having led him into bad company. He dreaded other reproaches still and was afraid of even personal violence. At last, one day in the summer of 1826, the uncle received the frightful news that his son had left his dwelling with a pair of pistols, and intended to take his own life. A long and terrible morning was spent searching for the unfortunate youth, who was finally led home, with a wound in his head, from Baden. "It's done now. Torment me no longer with reproofs and complaints," he writes; and his disposition and feeling may be inferred from the words found in his conversation leaves: "I have grown worse, because my uncle wanted to make me better;" and from these others: "He said it was not hatred, but a very different feeling, that moved him against you."

The uncle, alas! understood these expressions better than those about him. These had only words of reproach for the reprobate deed. "Evidences of the deepest pain were plainly to be seen in his bent attitude. The man, firm and upright in all the movements of his body, was gone. A person of about seventy was before us—yielding, without a will, the sport of every breath of air." So wrote Schindler. Beethoven called for the Bible "in the real language into which Luther had translated it." A few days later, we find in his conversations the following memorandum: "On the death of Beethoven." Did he mean his own death, or the death of the beloved boy with whom he had, so to speak, lost his own life? Be this as it may, he now sang the deepest song of his soul, and it was destined to be his dying song. We refer to the *adagio* in the last quartet, op. 135. His harp soon after this grew silent, and forever. Henceforth we have only projects or fragments of works. But he touched it once more, like King Gunther in the Edda, " seated among serpents," the most venomous of which—the pangs of his own conscience— menaced him with death. Among the pictures in which he paints the meaning of a theme similar to that of this *adagio* (pieces thus independent of one another cannot rightly be called variations), there is one whose minor key and rhythm show it to be a funeral ceremony of touching sublimity. But whatever guilt he may have incurred he atoned for in his heart of hearts by love. Such is this picture. His soul is free. This the theme itself tells us, eloquently and distinctly. Here the soul, in melancholy stillness, revolves about its own primeval source, and towards the close plumes its wing for a happy, lofty flight, to regions it has longed to enter. The other pictures show us this full, certain and joyful possession of one's self, and the last even seems to resolve the soul into its faculties when it floats about the Eternal Being in the most blissful happiness—a vision and condition which, of all the means of expression of the intellect, only music is able to describe, and which proves to us that, in the case of our artist, both fear and death had long been overcome.

And thus it comes that a movement with which there is none to be compared, one which to our feelings is the richest and most perfect of all movements, and, at the same time, of the most brilliant transparency, made its way into a work which otherwise shows no trace of the magnitude of this his last effort. For the *finale* is only a sham-play of those magic powers which our master so well knew how to conjure up, both in sublime horror and in saving joy.

But his physical condition was soon destined to be in keeping

The Schwarzspanierhaus ("House of the Black-robed Spaniards") in Vienna: the building in which Beethoven last lived and in which he died on March 26, 1827, at the age of 56. (Image/caption by the editor.)

with the condition of his soul above described. When, indeed, Karl was convalescing as well as could be desired, and he had decided to follow the military calling, Beethoven's friends noticed that, externally at least, he again looked fresh and cheerful. "He knew," says Schindler, "how to rise superior to his fate, and his whole character bore an 'antique dignity.'" But even now he told the old, friend of his youth, Wegeler, that he intended "to produce only a few more great works, and then, like an old child, to close his earthly career somewhere among good men." And, indeed, his whole inner nature seemed shattered. "What dost thou want? Why dost thou hang thy head? Is not the truest resignation, sufficient for thee, even if thou art in want?" This one conversation with Karl tells us everything.

Besides, serious symptoms of disease appeared. A single blow, and his powerful, manly form was shattered like that of the meanest of mortals. And, indeed, that blow was struck with almost unexpected violence.

After his recovery, Karl was released by the police on the express condition that he would remain in Vienna only one day more. His scar, however, prevented his entering the service. Where, then, could he go, now that the fall was just beginning? His brother, Johann, invited him to his Wasserhof estate near Gneixendorf. He could no longer answer as he had once: *non possibile per me*—impossible for me. But his sojourn in a country house not constructed so as to guard against the cold and dampness, a want of attention to his growing infirmity, misunderstandings with his brother's wife, a violent quarrel with the brother himself, who, after it, refused him the use of his close carriage, and, lastly, his departure in the cold of winter in the "devil's own worst conveyance." All these causes conspired to send our patient back to Vienna, the subject of a violent fit of sickness. In addition to all this, his nephew delayed to call a physician, and none visited his sick bed until the third day after his return. The doctor who came was not Beethoven's customary physician, and totally misunderstood the nature of the disease. Other shocks succeeded, and the consequence was a violent attack of dropsy, the symptoms of which had first shown themselves in Gneixendorf.

His long, painfully long end was now beginning. His constitution, powerful as that of a giant, "blocked the gates against death" for nearly three months. As labor of any kind was out of the question, the arrival of Handel's works from London, which came to him as a present, supplied him with the distraction he wished for, in his own sphere. It was not long before attacks of suffocation at night distressed him and it became necessary to perform the operation paracentesis. When he saw the stream of water gush forth, he remarked, with that sublimity of humor so peculiarly his own, that the surgeon reminded him of Moses, who struck the rock with his rod; but, in the same humorous vein, he added: "Better water from the stomach than from the pen." With this he consoled himself. But he grew worse, and a medical consultation seemed necessary to his friends. His own heart forebode him no good, and he again made his will on the 3rd of January, 1827. He made his beloved nephew "sole heir to all he possessed." The nephew had gone to join his regiment the day before, and this had a good and quieting effect on Beethoven. He knew that the young man would be best provided for there, and testified his gratitude to General von Stutterheim, who had received him, by dedicating to that officer his quartet in C sharp minor—his "greatest" quartet. He urged that Dr. Malfatti should be called. But he had had a falling out years before with him, and the celebrated physician did not now want to excite the displeasure of his colleagues. Schindler tells us: "Beethoven wept bitterly when I told him the doctor's decision."

But Malfatti came at last, and, after they had exchanged a few words, the old friends lay weeping in each other's arms. The doctor prescribed iced punch to "quicken the organs of digestion, enervated by too much medicine." The first physician who was called to attend him tells us: "The effect of the prescription was soon perceptible. He grew cheerful, was full of witty sallies at times, and even dreamt that he might be able to finish his oratorio *Saul and David*." From his written conversations, we see that a great many of his friends had gathered about his bed. He thought of finishing the Bach overture for one of Schindler's concerts, and even began to busy himself with the Tenth Symphony once more. He had again to experience the feeling of pecuniary embarrassment while in this condition—an embarrassment now more painful than ever—brought about more especially by the necessity of procuring a military outfit for Karl. Galitzin had, indeed, expressly promised a short time before to send him money, but he proved a "princely boaster;" and there was no prospect of an income from any other

After his death Beethoven's friends sent out this invitation to his funeral. (Image/caption by the editor.)

source. All his completed works had been sold, and the little fortune he had laid aside at the time of the Congress of Vienna was irrevocably pledged to Karl by his will.

His thoughts now turned to the "magnanimous" English, who

had already promised him a "benefit." His disease lasted a long time. The third operation had been performed. His long-continued solitude had alienated men from him in Vienna; and, especially after his experiences with the *Akademie* in 1824, he had no confidence in the devotion and enthusiasm for art of his second home. This induced Schindler to write to England: "But what afflicts him very much is, that no one here concerns himself in the least about him; and, indeed, this total absence of interest in him is very surprising." After this, we find only his most intimate friends at his bedside. Among these was Gleichenstein, who happened to be in Vienna on a short visit. He writes: "Thou must bless my boy as Voltaire blessed Franklin's son." Hummel, who was traveling and giving concerts, also saw him, and at the sight of his suffering—he had just undergone the fourth operation—burst into tears. Beethoven had, at the moment of Hummel's visit, received a little picture as a present, and he showed it to him, saying: "See, my dear Hummel, the house in which Haydn was born—the miserable peasant hut, in which so great a man was born!"

He asks his Rhenish publisher, Schott, who had purchased his Mass and his Ninth Symphony, and who was destined one day to become the owner of the *Niebelungen*, for some old wine to strengthen him. Malfatti recommended an aromatic bath; and such a bath, it seemed to him, would surely save him. But it had the very opposite effect, and he was soon taken with violent pains. He wrote to London: "I only ask God that I may be preserved from want as long as I must here endure a living death." The response was one thousand guldens from the Philharmonic Society of that city "on account of the concert in preparation." "It was heart-rending to see how he folded his hands and almost dissolved in tears of joy and gratitude" when he received them. This was his last joy, and the excitement it caused accelerated his end. His wound broke open again and did not close any more. He felt this at first a wonderful relief, and while he felt so he dictated some letters for London, which are among the most beautiful he has written. He promised to finish the Tenth Symphony for the Society, and had other "gigantic" plans, especially as regards his Faust-music. "That will be something worth hearing," he frequently exclaimed. The overflow of his fancy was "indescribable, and his imagination showed an elasticity which his friends had noticed but seldom when he was in health." At the same time, the most beautiful pictures of dramatic poetry floated before his mind, and in conversation he always represented his own works as filled with such "poetic ideas." But his sufferings soon became "indescribably great. His dissolution was approaching" with giant steps, and even his friends could only wish for his end. Schindler wrote to London on the 24th March: "He feels that his end is near, for yesterday he said to Breuning and me: "Clap your hands, friends; the play is over." And

Vincent d'Indy made this sketch of Beethoven's first tomb at the Cemetery at Währing (a district in Vienna) in 1880. (Image/caption by the editor.)

further: "He advances towards death with really Socratic wisdom and unexampled equanimity." He could well be calm of heart and soul. He had done his duty as an artist and as a man. This same day he wrote a codicil to his will in favor of his nephew; and now his friends had only one deep concern—to reconcile him with heaven. The physician approved, and Beethoven calmly but resolutely answered : "I will."

The clergyman came and Beethoven devoutly performed his last religious duties. Madame Johann van Beethoven heard him say, after he had received the Sacrament: "Reverend sir, I thank you. You have brought me consolation."

He then reminded Schindler of the letter to London. "May God bless them," he said. The wine he had asked for came. "Too bad!

too bad! it's too late!" These were his very last words. He fell immediately after into such an agony that he was not able to utter a single syllable more. On the 24th and 25th of March, the people came in crowds to see him again. Even the *faijaks*, Hoslinger and Holz, as well as the poet Castelli, were among them. "All three of us knelt before his bed," said Holz, subsequently, to Frau Linzbaur, who, in relating the incident, added that when Holz told it "his voice forsook him, and he covered his face and wept. 'He blessed us,' he said, with an effort; 'we kissed his hand, but never saw him again.'" This was the last act of his life.

"On the 26th, the little pyramidal clock, which he had received as a present from Princess Christiane Lichnowsky, stopped, as it still does when a storm is approaching. Schindler and Breuning had gone to the churchyard, to select a grave for him. A storm of loud thunder and hail came raging on about five o'clock. No one but Frau van Beethoven and the young composer, Anselm Huettenbrenner, who had hurried hither from Graz to look upon his revered master once more, were present in the room of the dying man. A stroke of lightning illuminated it with a lurid flash. The moribund opened his eyes, raised his right hand, and looked up with a fixed gaze for several seconds: the soul of the hero would not out. But "when his uplifted hand fell back on the bed, his eyes half closed. Not another breath! Not another heart-beat! It was I that closed the half-open eyes of the sleeper." So says Huettenbrenner, an eye-witness of our artist's last moment. This was the 26th of March, 1827.

"No mourning wife, no son, no daughter, wept at his grave, but a world wept at it." These are the words of the orator of the day on the occasion of the unveiling of the first monument to Beethoven in 1845, in Bonn. But his funeral on that beautiful day in spring was a very brilliant one. A sea of twenty thousand human beings surged over the street where now the votive church stands; for in the *Schwarzspanierhaus* behind it, Beethoven had lived during the last years of his life. The leading *capellmeisters* of the city carried the pall, and writers and musicians the torches.

"The news of his death had violently shaken the people out of their indifference," says Dr. G. von Breuning. And, indeed, it was, as a poor old huxtress exclaimed when she saw the funeral procession, "the general of musicians" whom men were carrying to the grave! The poet, Grillparzer, delivered the funeral oration. He took for his text the words: "He was an artist, and he was what he was only through his art." Our very being and our sublimest feelings are touched when we hear the name of

LUDWIG VAN BEETHOVEN.

(Image by the editor.)

MEET THE AUTHOR-EDITOR

NEO-VICTORIAN SCHOLAR LOCHLAINN SEABROOK, a descendant of the families of Alexander Hamilton Stephens, John Singleton Mosby, Edmund Winchester Rucker, and William Giles Harding, is a 7th generation Kentuckian and the most prolific pro-South writer in the world today. Known by literary critics as the "new Shelby Foote" and by his fans as the "Voice of the Traditional South," he is a recipient of the prestigious Jefferson Davis Historical Gold Medal. As a lifelong writer he has authored and edited books ranging in topics from history, politics, science, and biography, to nature, religion, music, and the paranormal, books that his readers describe as "game changers," "transformative," and "life altering."

One of the world's most popular living historians, he is a 17th generation Southerner of Appalachian heritage who descends from dozens of patriotic Revolutionary War soldiers and Confederate soldiers from Kentucky, Tennessee, North Carolina, and Virginia. A proud member of the Sons of the Confederate Veterans, he is a true Renaissance Man. Besides being an accomplished and well respected author-historian and Bible authority, he is also a Kentucky Colonel, eagle scout, screenwriter, nature, wildlife, and landscape photographer, artist, graphic designer, songwriter (3,000 songs), film composer, multi-instrument musician, vocalist, session player, music producer, genealogist, former history museum docent, and a former ranch hand, zookeeper, and wrangler.

His over 70 adult and children's books contain some 60,000 well-researched pages that have earned him accolades from around the globe. His works, which have sold on every continent except Antarctica, have introduced hundreds of thousands to vital facts that have been left out of our mainstream books. He has been endorsed internationally by leading experts, museum curators, award-winning historians, bestselling authors, celebrities, filmmakers, noted scientists, well regarded educators, TV show hosts and producers, renowned military artists, esteemed heritage organizations, and distinguished academicians of all races, creeds, and colors. Colonel Seabrook holds the world record for writing the most books on Southern icon Nathan Bedford Forrest: 12.

Of northern and central European descent, he is the 6th great-grandson of the Earl of Oxford and a descendant of European royalty. His modern day cousins include: Johnny Cash, Elvis Presley, Lisa Marie Presley, Billy Ray and Miley Cyrus, Patty Loveless, Tim McGraw, Lee Ann Womack, Dolly Parton, Pat Boone, Naomi, Wynonna, and Ashley Judd, Ricky Skaggs, the Sunshine Sisters, Martha Carson, Chet Atkins, Patrick J. Buchanan, Cindy Crawford, Bertram Thomas Combs (Kentucky's 50th governor), Edith Bolling (second wife of President Woodrow Wilson), Andy Griffith, Riley Keough, George C. Scott, Robert Duvall, Reese Witherspoon, Lee Marvin, Rebecca Gayheart, and Tom Cruise.

A constitutionalist and avid outdoorsman and gun advocate, Colonel Seabrook is the author of the international blockbuster, *Everything You Were Taught About the Civil War is Wrong, Ask a Southerner!* He lives with his wife and family in beautiful historic Middle Tennessee, the heart of the Confederacy.

For more information on author Mr. Seabrook visit

LOCHLAINNSEABROOK.COM

"How happy I am to be able to wander among bushes and herbs, under trees and over rocks; no man can love the country as I love it. . . . I never feel entirely well except when I am among scenes of unspoiled nature."

Ludwig van Beethoven